"The concept of mentalization – the ability to recr[...] the purpose of understanding oneself and others [...] in its contemporary form, although its origins are [...] of Elisa Galgut's book explains the concept masterfully, in a textbook lesson, relying on her knowledge of psychoanalysis and the philosophy of mind. The book then finds its groove, recruiting the concept of mentalization to revisit such literary stalwarts as Sophocles, Shakespeare, Milton, Yeats, and Austen. Here the innovation is to highlight the importance of literary form. Her readings are original, indeed pitch-perfect. The book is pleasure to read, wonderfully composed, and should be widely read."

Daniel Herwitz, *Fredric Huetwell Professor, Comparative Literature, Philosophy History of Art University of Michigan*

"In this interdisciplinary *tour de force* Galgut brings her philosophical, literary and psychoanalytic sensibilities magnificently together. Readable and gently scholarly, she argues that the formal structures of art and psychoanalysis both represent ways to contain and mentalise problematic feelings. In her analysis of Jane Austen's Free Indirect Discourse she shows how the combined voice of narrator and character entail a broadening and maturation of the self and its perspectives. As in psychoanalysis the dialogue of therapist and patient intertwine to build more meaningful narratives of people's lives, so in this lovely book Galgut summons literature and psychoanalysis into an aesthetically convincing duet. Essential reading for those interested in psychoanalysis, literature and their overlaps. In short, she, and her many insights sing satisfyingly true."

Prof Jeremy Holmes, MD FRCPsych, *psychoanalytic psychotherapist, University of Exeter, UK*

Mentalization and Literary Form

This book examines the ways in which literary form facilitates mentalization and our ability to be aware of our own and others' mental states, showing how we can use this awareness to make sense of our experiences and interactions.

Looking at narrative, the sonnet, free indirect speech, and autobiographical memory, Elisa Galgut focuses on the ways in which literary form not only contains difficult emotions, but how it shapes and develops these emotional states. She considers how the creative mind gives form to inchoate emotions and structures and processes them in ways that allow us to experience and give name to what was previously unclear and amorphous. Looking at the work of canonical figures of English literature, such as Shakespeare, Milton, and Austen, Galgut's focus on form – rather than content – offers the reader a novel way of understanding the ways in which literature engages our emotional lives.

Assuming no prior knowledge of complex psychoanalytic concepts, *Mentalization and Literary Form* is aimed at academic and graduate students focusing on literary studies and philosophy, as well as psychoanalysts interested in Literature.

Elisa Galgut is a poet and philosopher who teaches in the Philosophy Department at the University of Cape Town, South Africa. Her work focuses on the areas of the philosophy of psychoanalysis, and literary aesthetics.

Mentalization and Literary Form

Elisa Galgut

Routledge
Taylor & Francis Group

LONDON AND NEW YORK

Designed cover image: © Evheniia Vasylenko

First published 2026
by Routledge
4 Park Square, Milton Park, Abingdon, Oxon OX14 4RN

and by Routledge
605 Third Avenue, New York, NY 10158

Routledge is an imprint of the Taylor & Francis Group, an informa business

© 2026 Elisa Galgut

The right of Elisa Galgut to be identified as author of this work has been asserted in accordance with sections 77 and 78 of the Copyright, Designs and Patents Act 1988.

British Library Cataloguing-in-Publication Data
A catalogue record for this book is available from the British Library

ISBN: 978-1-032-70225-4 (hbk)
ISBN: 978-1-032-68562-5 (pbk)
ISBN: 978-1-032-70227-8 (ebk)

DOI: 10.4324/9781032702278

Typeset in Times New Roman
by Apex CoVantage, LLC

In memory of my parents, who encouraged my interest in the life of the mind.

Contents

Acknowledgements

I would like to thank the *Interdisciplinary Psychoanalytic Thought* research network, and in particular Dr Louise Braddock, for providing multiple fora over the years for stimulating discussions on psychoanalysis. The interdisciplinary nature of these engagements has offered fertile ground for the exploration of ideas at the intersection of psychoanalysis, literature, and philosophy.

Excerpts from *The Go-Between* by L.P. Hartley are reprinted with permission of Penguin Publishing. I also gratefully acknowledge The Society of Authors, as the Literary Representative of the Estate of L P Hartley, for permission to quote from the novel.

Introduction

This book brings together my three passions: philosophy, literature, and psychoanalysis. Because it is interdisciplinary, it is inevitable that certain issues will be highlighted and others sidelined. The main focus of the book is on the ways in which literary form facilitates our ability to reflect on ourselves. The concept of "the self" that I have in mind is a normative one, what philosophers call "a person". This term is not co-extensive with "human", which picks out a member of a biological species: a human is a creature that can be defined scientifically – it has a particular DNA, belongs to the species *Homo sapiens*, has an evolutionary history, and so on. The term "person" implies more than membership in a descriptive category. It is a concept of the self as agent who has free will, is fundamentally rational, and whose actions and judgements are made reasonable in the light of intentions that are formed by mental states such as beliefs and desires. A person also has ethical commitments which assist her in navigating life. Thus the term "person" is not reducible to "human"; not all humans are persons, and there may, at least conceivably, be persons that are not human.

It may seem as though the metaphysical view of persons does not matter that much for the sake of my discussion viewed narrowly, which is the ways in which literary form facilitates mentalization. But it matters for the bigger issue, because I understand my project as one that falls within a tradition of philosophy as a humanistic endeavour, and which shuns approaches to the self that seek to understand the mind mainly in terms of the brain or central nervous system. These projects are worthy scientific projects, but the philosophical self, to my mind, is not a scientific object. Another way of putting this is to say that I use the term "mind" as more or less synonymous with "person" – a being that thinks, understands, feels, cares about her will,[1] acts intentionally, and so on. Our self-understanding requires a personal-level account that involves stories about who we are. This philosophical tradition locates psychoanalysis within it, for the discoveries made by Freud and his followers belong to a discipline that does not only seek cure as its goal: it follows the Socratic legacy that searches for self-knowledge and understanding. Literature too forms part of this legacy: the stories we tell ourselves, about ourselves and for ourselves, are not merely for entertainment but flow from that same motivation to gain insight into who we are, and what motivates us to behave in certain ways.

DOI: 10.4324/9781032702278-1

Aristotle understood this when he claimed that the essence of tragedy is plot rather than character, for plot centres on action: who we are determines what we do, and conversely, our actions form what we become.

By saying that persons are essentially rational, I am not hereby denying those insights of psychoanalysis which posit that a core aspect of the self – what Freud called the dynamic unconscious – is irrational. But only rational beings can suffer from irrationality. If we were wholly or mainly irrational, we could not form an intention, hold a belief, or make a decision; in order to speak a language, we must understand that a word means one thing and not another, and we thus acknowledge the principle of non-contradiction, as well as other rules of logic. We explain our actions, to others and to ourselves, via narratives that invoke our reasons, beliefs, wishes, hopes, perspectives on the world, and so on. Our reason-governed behaviour breaks down, sometimes leading us mildly astray, sometimes in ways that create havoc and catastrophe. One of the aims of psychoanalysis is to explain the sources of such irrationality, and to suggest ways in which we can combat it. The focus of this book is not on the irrational that disrupts our lives, but rather on the ways in which those rational parts of the self can contribute to mindedness, thoughtful reflection, insight. The term that captures such minded activity is "mentalization". More narrowly, I focus on the ways in which literary form – and here my discussion must of necessity be narrow, given the plethora of ways in which writing can be presented to the reader – is tied to self-reflection.

The philosopher David Hume notes an analogy between befriending a person and befriending the author of a book: the author offers a perspective on the fictional world she creates, and we, the reader, are invited to engage with this perspective, usually by adopting it, but sometimes by challenging or questioning it. Engaging with a point of view is also what we do with other people. Perhaps there are more similarities between reading books and reading people for which mere metaphor allows. Although I am not arguing for a theory of mind that sees reading a book as *literally* reading the mind of another, it strikes me that Hume's analogy lies somewhere between metaphor and literal interpretation: reading books involves similar capacities, in certain respects, as does understanding the minds of others. The discussion that follows examines these connections. More narrowly, it examines the ways in which literature may facilitate or encourage mentalizing capacities. By "mentalizing capacities", I mean those abilities which enable us to understand our own and others' mental states, and to use this awareness to make sense of our own experiences and of our interactions with others. The term "mentalization" and its related verb "mentalizing" were introduced into the psychoanalytic/psychological literature in the 1960s and developed further by Peter Fonagy and his colleagues. We can think of the ability to mentalize "thinly" or "thickly"; on a thin interperion of the term, mentalization means "thinking about thinking" or "thinking about feeling" – the ability to develop metacognitive and meta-affective mental states.

This interpretation of mentalization requires little more than what (as we'll see in Chapter 1) philosophers call "theory of mind" or "folk psychology", which refers to the normal capacity to understand others and predict their behaviour. Such a capacity does not imply a deep awareness of another's emotional life, or a nuanced ability to perceive what they are thinking; it refers to the ordinary person's ability to engage with others, an ability that we mostly take for granted. On a thin reading of mentalization, most of us can mentalize well because we can form meta-representations of our own and others' mental states. Many of these mentalizing abilities are automatic, and we rely on them on a daily basis to navigate the world around us: we make arrangements to see friends, anticipating where and when they will meet with us based on the previous day's discussion; we predict what an erratic driver may do at an intersection, and we avoid engaging with an angry person in anticipation that he or she may not respond to our overtures with patience or understanding. Mentalization understood in this "thin" sense is certainly important, but the real significance of the concept, especially for psychoanalysis, resides in a "thick" understanding of the term. Here, the ability to mentalize involves not only the capacity to form metacognitive states, but it requires something more – a sensitivity to others, a nimbleness of mind, an ability to process one's own emotional states in ways that allow for psychological growth and depth. This thick understanding of the concept situates mentalization firmly within a psychoanalytic picture of the mind: a person with mature mentalizing capacities has an ordered inner world that is not dominated by primitive defence mechanisms such as projection or splitting; she is able to tolerate frustration, to think before acting or "acting out", and displays a willingness to consider different perspectives. Mentalization-based treatments[2] have been used to assist those with disorders such as borderline personality, as it has proven effective in helping patients to refrain from impulsive behaviours, for example, and in "bridging the gap between affects and their representation" (Bateman and Fonagy 2004, 203).

The argument of this book is that reading certain kinds of literature requires or facilitates mentalizing capacities. I use the terms "requires or facilitates" because I am open to various possibilities regarding the ways in which book reading and mind reading are connected: reading may *facilitate* our mentalizing capacities, help develop them, or simply require them. I am sure that the relationship between literary engagement and the development of mentalizing skills is nuanced and complex, and almost certainly tied to psychological development. There seems to be good evidence that reading storybooks facilitates mentalizing skills in children and thus plays an important role in children's cognitive and emotional development. The focus of this book is less on the educational role of literature and more on the ways in which reading may enhance our abilities to reflect on our emotional lives and develop our capacity for reflection by requiring or facilitating metacognitive and meta-affective thinking skills. I am not claiming that we necessarily identify with the characters in a story and mentalize in virtue of seeing things from their perspective, as some recent work[3] on simulation theory[4] suggests. Sometimes we may identify with a character in ways that enable us to mentalize with her, but such identification is neither necessary nor sufficient for mentalization. I shall say a little more about this in Chapter 2.

Because I regard literature as a humanistic endeavour, my views here may run counter to those who see texts as divorced from the person who writes them, who see texts as opportunities for open-ended interpretations that are unconcerned with the exigencies of everyday life. Of course, this does not mean that I do not think that literature can explore fantasy worlds, or involve non-human characters, or must always engage with fundamental questions of human existence. But I do hold that literature that stands the test of time concerns itself with issues that are of fundamental concern to our quest to understand ourselves. This view is echoed by psychoanalysts Hanna Segal and Ronald Britton. Segal,[5] for example, distinguishes between *as-if* fantasy fiction, which "is pure escapism, making even day-dreaming easy, since someone else has made the effort to plot it", and *what-if* fiction, which requires "imagining what would happen if some parameter were changed. . . . This kind of imagination does not deny reality to produce an 'as-if' world, but explores possibilities" (Segal 1991, 107). Britton[6] distinguishes serious from pulp fiction by arguing that the latter is escapist and avoids engagement with genuine emotions, while the former

"resonates with something unconscious and profoundly evocative" and is ultimately more likely "to be recognised by the critically enlightened".

(Britton 1998, 113)

He argues that much of the emotional power of great fiction lies in its ability to evoke and work through unconscious phantasy. My focus in the book is on mentalization and literary form, which is a change of focus rather than a change of topic.

Unlike other works[7] on the relationship between literature and psychoanalysis, the focus of my book is on literary form rather than content, although of course they are importantly interrelated. However, because there has been very little discussion on the ways in which *formal* elements of literature facilitate mentalization, my book is an attempt to fill this gap. I am interested in the ways in which literary form not only *contains* (sometimes difficult) emotions but also how it shapes and develops these emotional states. Wordsworth noted that poetry is "emotion recollected in tranquillity", but such recollections involve more than remembering – the creative mind gives form to inchoate emotions, and shapes and processes them in ways that allow us to experience and give name to what was previously unclear and amorphous. Literary form in the hands of a great writer, such as Shakespeare, Milton, or Jane Austen, enables new ways of understanding our emotional lives, and a discussion on *form*, rather than *content*, can, I hope, illustrate some of these ways. I do not mean my study to be either exhaustive or prescriptive – two different poets may, for example, use the sonnet form to different ends, and great literature is characterized by inventiveness that can never be captured in rules. Nevertheless, form is vital not only for structuring content, but for shaping it: *how* something is expressed changes *what* is expressed. The same story expressed via different forms will be altered by the way it is told: a love poem in haiku form will tell a very different kind of story from the same content written as a sonnet. Form is not a garment that merely adorns a body; it is more like skin than clothing, an essential element of a work of art which constitutes, in part, its very nature, and determines its meaning. My book focuses on a few examples of form, and thus of necessity involves cherry-picking: I am not claiming that the literary forms discussed in the following chapters are the *only* ways in which mentalizing capacities are facilitated. I regard my discussion as an exploration, the beginning of a project that, hopefully, others may find interesting and in which they may participate.

The outline of the book is as follows: in Chapter 1, I introduce the notion of mentalization as coined by psychoanalysts Pierre Marty and Pierre Luquet in France, and later by Peter Fonagy, Mary Target, György Gergely, and Elliot Jurist. Mentalization, the capacity to understand and predict the behaviour of others and ourselves, is understood within a psychoanalytic view of the mind more generally. I locate mentalization at the heart of self-understanding, and I discuss the concept more fully. This chapter also examines psychoanalysis as an extension of folk psychology; I argue that folk psychology – the term used to refer to the ways in which we all, commonly, understand the mind – involves the use of narrative explanation. The philosopher Donald Davidson argues that mental explanation is essentially about providing reasons for our actions. Reasons *explain* why we act, and allow us to understand, from the agent's point of view, why he behaved in a certain way. I examine the role of narrative as being central to psychological explanation, as unpacking the *why* of human behaviour. Narrative lies at the core of our understanding of ourselves as agents, beings who act with intention. When we engage in the project of understanding ourselves and others, we do so via storytelling: B happens because of A, which then leads to the occurrence of C. Essentially, narratives make sense of behaviour, and it is this "making sense" that also lies at the heart of psychoanalysis. Freud postulated a dynamic unconscious because, by doing so, he was able to explain the behaviour of his patients that would otherwise have remained inexplicable – to themselves as well as to observers.

In this chapter I also defend the use of mentalization as part of *psychoanalytic* explanation more widely: some critics argue that mentalization is not a psychoanalytic concept because it does not necessarily refer to the dynamic unconscious. I understand mentalization within a broad view of psychoanalysis; the notion of mentalization *emphasizes* mental abilities that are involved in understanding the self and the other. Focuses on the ways in which literary form facilitates mentalization, I embed this focus in a wider view of the psychoanalytic mind.

In Chapter 2, I focus on literary form. Most psychoanalytic writings on art and literature emphasize the ways in which unconscious conflict is expressed in literature, especially via its content. This chapter explores the importance of form in shaping meaning in literary works. Psychoanalytically, form can function as a container, holding and shaping painful emotions, and this aspect of form will be examined more fully in Chapter 3 (The Sonnet). I explore how literary form differs from the *mere* provision of a narrative. This distinction is first provided by Aristotle in his emphasis on the importance of plot in tragedy; Aristotle distinguishes *plot* from other kinds of narratives by arguing that plot, via its structure, shows the causal relationship between events. Aristotle also points out that certain plots are better suited to tragedy insofar as they provide a certain kind of emotional resolution. Aristotle is interested in *katharsis* as a *tragic* emotion, but of course different literary forms (and contents) will give rise to different kinds of emotional responses. The key issue examined in this chapter is the nature of literary form and its importance with regard to emotional responses in literature.

In Chapter 3, I examine poetic form as another way in which the formal elements of literature enable mentalization. The sonnet, with its tight structure and lyric form, gives us, in the words of literary critic Helen Vendler, "the mind alone with itself".[8] The sonnet is one of the oldest prescribed poetic forms. Strictness of form primes a reader's expectations and enables complex and often difficult emotions to be contained in ways that bring insight and enable mentalization. The tight structure of the sonnet is able to convey the development of thought, and its brevity allows the reader to follow and keep in mind at a single reading changes in ideas and emotional affect. The sonnet form is thus in a unique position for both depicting and exemplifying the thinking process. I examine a few sonnets in detail, illustrating how the sonnet form works to enable the processing of complex emotions.

Chapter 4 focuses on Jane Austen's use of free indirect discourse, which is the literary technique whereby the first-person thoughts of a character are written in the grammatical third person. I show that Austen's writing facilitates the development of mentalization by providing a multilayered reading that allows the reader to see a situation from multiple perspectives. This allows the novelist to present different viewpoints of characters, as well as the comments of the novelist *on* the characters, without allowing the authorial voice to dominate. Free indirect discourse allows the narrative flow to remain uninterrupted as it directs the reader's gaze without drawing attention to itself. It further requires that the reader develop a finely attuned ear in order to pick up the subtleties of the text. I examine examples of free indirect discourse, and the various ways it can be put to use, with references to selected passages from *Persuasion*, *Emma*, and *Pride and Prejudice*. As with all the particular literary works discussed, these examples are illustrative of Austen's skills and are not meant as either definitive or conclusive of the ways in which Austen's use of literary technique may be used to facilitate mentalizing capacities. Indeed, given Austen's genius, such an examination would require a book on its own.

The final chapter explores the relationship between mentalization and autobiographical memory. Autobiographical memory grounds a person's sense of identity: it creates a narrative about the self from episodic memories about specific times and places. Autobiographical memory fosters the autobiographical self as it weaves autobiographical memories together in a meaningful way. I propose that advanced capacities for mentalization alter autobiographical memory, and mentalized memory is associated with certain formal properties that are lacking in non-mentalized memory. I examine the ways in which these formal elements of autobiographical memory are developed and examined via literary form.

In this chapter, I examine three different pieces of literature. First, I analyse Yeats's "The Wild Swans at Coole", an autobiographical poem which reflects the poet's capacities for autobiographical memory that exhibits mentalizing capacities. The poem is imbued with emotional resonance gained from insight, and Yeats weaves together experiences of the past and present to provide meaning about a future in which he will be absent. The poem is in part an exploration of the role of memory. I then discuss L.P. Hartley's novel *The Go-Between*, in which the narrator, Leo, fails to understand fully the events of his past and ends up repeating them. The novel is written as autobiographical memory, as the adult Leo revisits his past, but it is also about memory, and the ways in which memory may lead us astray rather than bring insight or understanding. It is not that Leo misremembers, but he fails to understand fully the import of certain events in his past and, by failing to remember correctly, is doomed to repeat them. I then read the play where the three roads of philosophy, psychoanalysis and literature meet – Sophocles' *Oedipus*. The play reminds us that an autobiographical narrative – no matter how seemingly coherent – may not be the true narrative of who we really are: seemingly coherent narratives may conceal more than they reveal. I extend this discussion regarding the ways in which narrative style may be exploited to conceal, rather than clarify, our motivations via Richard Wollheim's analysis of Freud's case study of the Rat Man. Wollheim, following Freud, claims that the Rat Man's narrative misrepresents his true motivation so that his actions appear more intelligible than they really are. Wollheim points out that narrative is the vehicle by which unconscious phantasy is disguised as ordinary desire, which can then function in the explanation of an action. The Rat Man places himself as an actor in his own story, and so, rather than feeling at the mercy of unwelcome and uncontrollable phantasies, he becomes – or seems to become – an agent who acts by deliberation. Wollheim probes the connections between narrative and phantasy and its vicissitudes and shows how behaviour motivated by unconscious phantasy can appear to be more rational when it yokes itself to the cause-and-effect structure of narrative explanation.

The book concludes with an exploration of the limits of narrative. Because unconscious phantasy is structured in accordance with the pleasure principle and primary processing, it cannot directly give rise to intentional action but must be mediated via secondary processing and the reality principle. But the unconscious uses the features of narrative to enable a kind of acting out that is nevertheless ego-syntonic. Perhaps another way of expressing the idea of this chapter is as follows: in the main, my book understands psychoanalysis as an extension of ordinary folk psychology, and I argue that literary form plays a key role in shaping our mentalizing capacities. In other words, I have argued that the formal elements of literature provide ways of understanding ourselves. Because narrative explains how and why we act, we use it to explain our *rational conscious* selves. It thus also makes sense that we use narrative to understand our *irrational* selves, even where such explanations ultimately fit uncomfortably, like badly made clothes on the human form. The final discussion thus examines the ways in which narrative can make irrational activity appear more like rational action; if this is so, we must be on our guard to distinguish genuine explanation from sophistic rationalization. This is, perhaps, another contribution that literature makes to both philosophy and psychoanalysis: by understanding more about the ways in which form can facilitate mentalization, we can develop skills that can also enable us to distinguish true from false insight, and ways of reading that lead to understanding from misreadings that lead us astray. Literature, psychoanalysis, and philosophy are art forms: interpretation is an activity, a form of becoming rather than a way of being. Plato understood this when he depicted Socrates as engaging in conversation. Psychoanalysis and literature are also ways in which we can engage in conversation with another: book reading is a form of mind reading.

Notes

1 I borrow this term from Harry Frankfurt; see "Freedom of the Will and the Concept of a Person", *The Journal of Philosophy* 68, no. 1 (1971): 5–20.
2 See, for example, Anthony W. Bateman and Peter Fonagy, *Psychotherapy for Borderline Personality Disorder: Mentalization-Based Treatment* (Oxford University Press, 2004).
3 See, for example, Kendall Walton, "Fearing Fictionally", *The Journal of Philosophy* 75, no. 1 (1978): 5–27; Gregory Currie, "Imagination and Simulation: Aesthetics Meets Cognitive Science", in *Mental Simulation*, eds. Martin Davis and Tony Stone (Blackwell, 1995): 151–169; Aaron Meskin and Jonathan M. Weinberg, "Emotions, Fiction, and Cognitive Architecture", *British Journal of Aesthetics* 43, no. 1 (2003): 18–34.
4 Simulation theory is a theory about the nature of folk psychology which claims that our ability to explain and predict the behaviour of others is in virtue of the functional similarity between ourselves and the other person. We use ourselves as a model in explaining their behaviour. Simulation theory stands in contrast to the so-called "Theory Theory" view of folk psychology.
5 Hanna Segal, "Imagination, Play and Art", in *Dream, Phantasy and Art* (Brunner-Routledge, 1991): 101–109.
6 Ronald Britton, "Daydream, Phantasy and Fiction", in *Belief and Imagination: Explorations in Psychoanalysis* (Brunner-Routledge, 1998): 109–119.
7 See, *inter alia*, Ernst Jones, *"The Problem of Hamlet and the Oedipus-Complex" – An Introductory Essay to Shakespeare's Hamlet* (Vision Press, 1947); Hamish Canham and Carole Satyamurti, eds., *Acquainted with the Night: Psychoanalysis and the Poetic Imagination* (Routledge, 2003); Inge Wise and Maggie Mills, eds., *Psychoanalytic Ideas and Shakespeare* (Karnac, 2006).
8 Helen Vendler, *The Art of Shakespeare's Sonnets* (Harvard University Press, 1997): 19.

Chapter 1

The Structure of Mind

Narrative, Folk Psychology, and Mentalization

In his *Poetics*, Aristotle observed that plot is the soul of tragedy. Although he refers specifically to tragic drama, his observation can be extended to literature more generally, and, ultimately, to the sphere of lived human activity. Aristotle considers tragedy to be the summit of literary achievement, and the literary arts in turn are important because they contain essential truths about human nature. Aristotle emphasizes the importance of the *plot*, which lies at the heart of action, and so of life: "For Tragedy is an imitation, not of men, but of an action and of life, and life consists in action."[1] But not just any story constitutes a plot; Aristotle emphasizes that events in tragedy happen not merely sequentially, but causally: it's not sufficient that B follows A (*post hoc*) – plot requires that B happens *because of* A (*propter hoc*). A plot captures more than a sequence of events; it provides the characters' reasons for behaving the way they do. E.M. Forster famously captures this difference by saying that a story is "a narrative of events arranged in their time-sequence", whereas a plot

> is also a narrative of events, the emphasis falling on causality. "The king died and then the queen died" is a story. "The king died, and then the queen died of grief" is a plot. The time-sequence is preserved, but the sense of causality overshadows it.[2]

A plot not only captures *what* happens but explains *why* it happens. The *why* lies at the heart of human activity: we act for reasons, and these reasons help us make sense of our own lives as well as the lives of others. For Aristotle, plot centred around action rather than character because, as philosopher Deborah Knight[3] notes, "we only come to understand characters in the context of either small-scale or larger-scale actions in which they participate. The test of character, we might say, is what one does when action is called for" (Knight 67). The emphasis on action, then, is not to deny the importance of the actor or agent, but rather to indicate that we come to agency via our actions: what we do influences who we are. Another important aspect of agency is that of perspective: in order to understand why Hamlet and Oedipus behave the way they do, we need to see the world through their eyes: "Actions can be made sense of if we can think of them as plausible under the circumstances" (Knight 67),

DOI: 10.4324/9781032702278-2

and plausibility is cashed out via the agent's point of view. An action might seem irrational or undesirable under one description, but reasonable under another: we may find it strange that Phoebe chooses to swim on cold winter days in outdoor rather than indoor pools until we learn that she is training for a long-distance swim and wants to acclimatize to cold conditions. Narratives capture not only the sequence of events, but the reasons and motivations that lie at the heart of human behaviour.

Narrative underscores psychological explanation too; intentional action would be incomprehensible without appealing to such *why* explanations. Knight argues that the commonsense aspect of folk psychology can be attributed to its narrative nature: "Psychological explanation enjoys this ubiquity", she writes, "because it is a narrative-based, agent-centred interpretive practice" (Knight 64). Reasons and motivations provide a way of understanding why a person acted the way she did; they do not merely show *that* her actions were causally responsible for subsequent events, but *how* and *why* they led to such events. Knight claims that the narrative nature of interpretation is a key feature of psychological explanation: a central agent or protagonist relates a course of action or events to a listener or audience from a particular point of view or perspective in order to show the "level of connexity" between events. By "connexity", Knight argues that events in a narrative are linked not only by causality but are "represented in terms of anticipations of future happenings and as retrospections concerning what has happened in the past" (Knight 70). A successful understanding of a narrative is when the listener or audience is able to make "*further correct interpretations* of an ongoing course of action" (Knight 64, italics in original). This chimes with the analysis of plot outlined earlier: narrative unpacks the *why* of human behaviour. The aim of narrative is communication, and this assumes a shared social world and a shared psychology. Knight makes the important point that narratives not only are about understanding the actions of agents, but they provide an avenue for exploring their emotional and intellectual lives. There is all the difference in the world between knowing that Oedipus intentionally killed an old man at the crossroads but unintentionally killed his father, even though the old man was his father, and knowing that Oedipus intentionally killed his father, the old man at the crossroads. The former, but not the latter, is the fabric of tragedy. We cannot fully understand Oedipus' actions without understanding his intentions – his inner world as reflected in his outer actions. Another important element of narratives to which Knight draws our attention is the role of the narrator: events are told from someone's perspective to an audience, usually (although not always, especially with regard to unreliable narrators of various kinds) to make the events intelligible to the listener or reader. As we'll see in Chapter 4 on Jane Austen, perspective is crucial for intelligibility: perspective suggests to the audience how a character's thoughts or actions should be understood. Sometimes – as in the case of a reliable omniscient narrator – the perspective may become invisible: what the narrator tells us is how things are. But sometimes we are invited to think about the intentions of the narrator herself and interpret the narrated events via a narratorial perspective that may be skewed or unreliable in some way or other. More is said about this in later chapters.

A central difference between folk psychological accounts of behaviour that place agency and intentionality at the centre of the narrative, and explanations that involve descriptions of mere causality, can be illustrated in the following way. If we are told that Marlie is depressed because her serotonin levels are low, or that she fell off a mountain because she slipped on the wet rocks, these explanations tell us a *causal* story, and they do not include information about Marlie's *reasons* for acting. This is not because the explanations are simple or sparse – we could expand the accounts by including information about the amount of rain on the rocks, for example, or give a detailed analysis explaining the interaction of serotonin with other neurotransmitters and how this influences affective states. These expanded accounts would not change the *nature* of the explanations, however; they would remain as objective causal accounts. To put it another way, these explanations would hold, generally speaking, for *anyone* in Marlie's situation. If Oscar or Phoebe walked on the same slippery rocks, it is very likely that they too would fall off the mountain; and if low serotonin tends to cause depression, this will be true not only of Marlie but of Oscar and Phoebe too. Of course, there will be relevant individual differences – if Oscar wears mountain boots that aid his grip, this will assist in preventing a fall, or there may be factors in Phoebe's genetics that safeguard her against depression, but these differences are not *personal* in the sense that they are not related to Marlie, Oscar, or Phoebe as persons or agents, with their individual tastes, likes, and dislikes. Had Marlie worn hiking boots like Oscar's, with the extra grip, she too may have avoided slipping on the rocks. Note also that the aforementioned behaviours are describable from a third-person perspective; the first-person point of view is either not germane or central to an explanation of behaviour that is fundamentally about objective causes.

On the other hand, agent-centred explanations that lie at the heart of psychology focus not on causes, but on reasons. This is not to deny, of course, that our reasons cause our actions, but the causal force is of an entirely different nature from the types in the earlier examples. For one thing, as Donald Davidson[4] famously argues, psychological causes, unlike physical ones, are not subsumable under general causal laws. The mental is anomalous – it is not governed by laws. The main reason to account for the fact that there are no psychological laws that explain human behaviour is because in an agent-centred explanation, the focus is on the person's reasons for acting from *her* point of view, and her reasons may be unique to her and impossible to generalize to others. As Davidson[5] notes, we cannot compare psychological truisms, such as "if a man wants to eat an acorn omelette, then he generally will if the opportunity exists and no other desire overrides" (Davidson 2001, 191), with a law of physics, such as Newton's laws of motion. The analogy between psychological and physical generalizations does not hold because "in the latter case, but not the former, we can tell in advance whether the condition holds, and we know what allowance to make if it doesn't" (Davidson 191). There may be a myriad of reasons why a man may fail to eat an acorn omelette despite wishing to do so, and these reasons are *in principle* impossible to stipulate in advance without knowing the detailed particulars of his case. The man may wish to eat an acorn omelette because he believes it would be healthy for him, but he dislikes omelettes. He may wish to eat an acorn omelette to win a bet but finds this is an insufficient reason to motivate him to go through with it. He may mistakenly believe that acorns are almonds. The same holds for Marlie's states of mind: if she is psychologically depressed, it will be for reasons applicable to her and her alone. Even if there are factors related to depression that are generalizable to others (the impact of traumatic events on states of mind, say), in order to understand why *Marlie* is depressed, we need to know the specificities of *her* situation. Perhaps her beloved dog died. Perhaps she failed an important exam. Perhaps she *passed* an important exam, but has imposter syndrome and feels she doesn't deserve to excel at her studies. Explanations about Marlie that involve her beliefs, desires, intentions, emotions, and other mental states are known as "folk psychological" or "common-sense" explanations because they are the kinds of explanations that "we, the folk" give of ourselves and others so routinely that we are not even aware we are doing anything special. Folk psychological explanations of behaviour are commonsensical and commonplace. Explanations such as "Alice believes it will rain today so she'll take her umbrella to work" or "Bob will boil the kettle because he enjoys a cup of warm coffee on a cold morning" are folk psychological accounts – they appeal to Alice and Bob's states of mind to explain and predict their behaviour.

Folk psychology is also sometimes referred to as "intentional psychology" precisely because it appeals to a person's beliefs, desires, and intentions to explain his or her behaviour. We use such folk psychological accounts all the time – to explain our behaviour to others, and theirs to ourselves. We also use folk psychology to explain our own behaviour to ourselves. Folk psychology is such an integral part of how we negotiate the social world that we are, for the most part, unaware of how deeply entrenched it is. To quote the philosopher Jerry Fodor, "commonsense psychology works so well it disappears".[6] We appeal to a person's beliefs, desires, wants, and intentions so often that we are mostly unaware that this is what we *are* doing; it is usually only when a person's behaviour is mysterious to us that we will *explicitly* think about the reasons that may have caused her to act as she did. Regarding our own behaviour, if we act in ways that are opaque to ourselves, this often triggers a mental breakdown of some kind, and we search out psychological help if we are unable to understand the reasons that motivated us to act: irrationality begins where folk psychological explanation ends.

Personal-Level Explanation

Commonsense psychology operates at the so-called "personal level". The term was coined by the philosopher Daniel Dennett, who made a distinction between personal-level explanations and sub-personal-level explanations. At the personal level, "explanations proceed in terms of the needs, desires, intentions and beliefs of an actor in an environment".[7] To emphasize the unique nature of personal-level explanation, which is second nature to us and so it may seem almost surprising to demarcate it via a distinct concept, Dennett contrasts it with the sub-personal level, which refers to explanations at the level "of brains and events in the nervous system" (Dennett, 93). The sub-personal level appeals to physical or biological explanations, where behaviour is cashed out in terms of cause-and-effect. To explain Marlie's depression in terms of low serotonin uptake would be a sub-personal explanation, as is a cognitive psychological account of the workings of short-term memory, or the nature of language acquisition, or the mechanisms of perception. Such accounts refer to *aspects* of persons, not persons as wholes, and they are amenable to third-person description. Personal-level explanations, on the contrary, refer to persons as agents whose perspectives are essential to understanding their behaviour. Commonsense psychology is the psychology of persons. It is somewhat misleading, though, to say that personal-level explanations offer a unique perspective on human behaviour. This understates the case, because it leaves open the possibility that there may be other ways of making sense of our lives – perhaps by appealing to competing theories that might one day even replace folk psychology. There are philosophers[8] who have suggested that someday a scientific psychology may replace our ordinary ways of talking about and understanding ourselves. What such a psychology would look like is opaque to us: it lies beyond dreamland, for even our dreams involve beliefs, desires, longings, emotions, and all the stuff central to folk psychology.

Folk Psychology as Constitutive

Folk psychology is irreplaceable as an account of human behaviour not only because it is the best available *explanation* of our mentality, but because it *constitutes* such mentality. What does this mean? In simple terms, it means that the way we think about our minds constitutes, in part, the nature of the mind itself. Let's take Miranda's belief that there is a cup of coffee on the kitchen table. In order for Miranda to have this belief, she must also have a concept of belief. She may not be able to articulate explicitly the nature of this concept – it may be tacit, but it is operative. For instance, Miranda knows that beliefs track the truth: if she discovers that the cup contains tea rather than coffee, she will adjust her belief, and acknowledge her former belief was wrong – she was mistaken. Beliefs are truth-sensitive, and part of what it means to hold beliefs is that one is aware of their truth-sensitive nature, of the conditions under which our beliefs succeed or fail in representing the world to us. We realize that beliefs can be false. If Miranda were the kind of person who thought that her beliefs were infallible, she would be puzzled to discover that the cup contains tea. Perhaps she would be led into self-deception: if the cup holds tea, and if beliefs are infallible, then Miranda may believe that she *always* believed the cup held tea. Children younger than about three years of age have a concept of belief along these lines: they believe, falsely, that beliefs do not present a picture *of* the world, but rather mirror the world. Gopnik and Wellman[9] note that a representational concept of belief is a developmental achievement:

> Two-year-olds have an early theory that is incorrect in that it does not posit the existence of mental representational states, prototypically beliefs. In 3-year-olds there is an intermediate phase where children demonstrate an understanding of the existence of representational states, at times, but only as auxiliary hypotheses.
>
> (Gopnik and Wellman, 150)

Only when children are about four years of age do they develop a theory of mind and understand that beliefs are mental states that indicate an agent's thoughts *about* the world rather than simply reflecting how the world is. Thus two-year-old children fail to understand that a belief may be false, and this leads to incorrect predictions about both their own and others' states of mind. As evidence for this, Gopnik and Wellman cite what's known as "the false belief test",[10] in which children are asked to predict where Minnie will look for the chocolate bar that she placed in the cupboard drawer, but which, unbeknownst to her, Mickey has stolen and placed in his backpack. Children younger than three tend to predict that Minnie will look in Mickey's backpack for the chocolate bar, while children of four and older predict that Minnie will look in the drawer, the place she hid it. This reflects the difference in their concept of belief: if, as for younger children, beliefs mirror the world, then Minnie will search for the chocolate where it is, whereas older children recognize that there is a difference between the way the world is and the way that we *represent* the world. Older children can distinguish between a fact and its presentation and understand that two people may think differently about the same state of affairs.

Thus the ways in which we understand our own mental states will determine, at least in part, their nature and function. Imagine, perhaps, that Miranda is *confused* about the nature of her mental states, and thinks that her *wish* that the cup contains coffee functions like a *belief*. This will cause her to behave in ways that are mistaken. She may, for instance, wonder why the tea (which she thinks is coffee) looks insipid and tastes so bland, and she may resolve not to buy that particular brand again. What this shows is that having beliefs requires that we also have a *concept* of the nature of belief:[11] false mental state concepts lead to false beliefs about ourselves. Another way of putting this is to say that there is an element of self-representation in the constitution of the mental. And concepts such as belief, intention, desire, and so on are the language of folk psychology – the way we understand ourselves and others and explain our behaviour. In the realm of folk psychology thinking does, in this sense, make it so. We are able to explain and predict the behaviour of others because we employ the language and concepts of folk psychology, without which "we wouldn't have any purchase on the idea of significant behaviour in the first place, let alone be able to decide what sorts of behaviours stand in need of explanation" (Knight 66).

Folk Psychology: Theory or Simulation?

There has been debate in the philosophy of psychology regarding the nature of folk psychology: is it a theory, or do we understand others by taking ourselves as a model, "simulating" their thoughts such that we imagine what we would do were we in their situation? An in-depth discussion of this debate will take me beyond the perimeters of the core discussion of this book, but I do want to distinguish what I am doing from some recent work in aesthetics concerning our engagement with fictional characters, which appeals to this discussion. In the 1970s, the philosopher Colin Radford[12] argued that our emotional engagement with fictional characters is irrational because we know that such characters do not exist. Radford appeals to a cognitive theory of emotions, which argues that emotions require beliefs, and he claims that we should not feel emotions towards people or situations that we know are fictional. Weeping over the fate of Anna Karenina, for example, is incoherent because we know that there is no such person in the real world. No one *actually* dies when we read of Anna's suicide in the novel, and we as readers know this, but we weep all the same. This claim generalizes to all fictional characters: we ought not loathe Iago, fear for Lear at the hands of his two oldest daughters, or hope that Elizabeth Bennet and Darcy will marry and find happiness.

Radford's paper generated a cottage industry of responses from philosophers who disagree with Radford, and who wanted to defend the commonsensical view that we *do* feel for fictional characters, that there is nothing wrong with doing so, and that reading fiction is nonsensical without acknowledging this. Some of these responses make reference to simulation theory as a way of solving Radford's puzzle. The argument goes something like this: we understand and predict the behaviour of others in virtue of simulating them, not by appealing to a theory about human psychology. Just as we might predict the flight pattern of an aeroplane by building a model rather than by mathematical calculation with reference to the laws of physics, so we understand others by using ourselves as a model rather than by applying a general theory about human behaviour. We "simulate" them: we put ourselves in their position and imagine what we ourselves would do if confronted with a similar predicament. Since we are like them in relevant respects, how *we* would behave gives us a good sense of how *they* would behave. Such behaviour may involve action, but it would also involve beliefs and emotions: I can predict that Billy will be happy to know that he has won first prize in the violin competition because *I* would be overjoyed if *I* won first prize for my violin competition. When Sherlock Holmes tries to figure out where the butler Brunton looked for the buried treasure,[13] he imagines himself in Brunton's position, attributes to himself the beliefs and desires of the butler, and then tries to predict how Brunton behaved. Thus Holmes's practical reasoning system processes information and makes inferences in the usual way, but instead of reasoning about his own beliefs and desires, he takes as input the beliefs and desires of Brunton. The resultant of this decision procedure allows Holmes to predict the behaviour of the butler not in virtue of the application of a theory, but by running a simulation.

This works too for fictions: when we read, we imagine that we are like the characters in the fictional world, and we take their beliefs as input. Because we are engaging with fictions and not real-life characters, the output of this simulation is not behaviour on our part, but rather beliefs, desires, and emotions. Our ability to simulate fictional characters happens at the sub-personal level; it is largely unconscious and automatic. The writer does her part by presenting us with a fictional world that facilitates the simulation. As Meskin and Weinberg write regarding our emotional responses concerning Anna Karenina:

> When I read that some horrible misfortune has befallen Anna, that simulated belief can activate my affect systems just as it would if I had a real belief that an actual person has suffered such a misfortune. Thus my emotional response is appropriately robust.
>
> (Meskin and Weinberg 2003, 24)

The further the fiction from the real world, the more difficult will be the simulation, and we may find that fictional worlds that are very unlike ours may require greater effort on the reader's part to engage the simulation.

I shall not discuss the merits or problems of simulation theory as a response to the question of how we have emotional responses to fictions. My concern is to distinguish my claims about reading and mentalization from the simulation approach. In this book, I do not take a position regarding the simulation/theory-theory debate; although I do tacitly endorse a position that sees both folk psychology and psychoanalysis as theories about the mind, I am open to the possibility that at least some of the ways in which we think about others may be along the lines that the simulationists suggest. It may even be that, in practice, aspects of mentalizing skills involve simulation. My discussion of mentalization, however, is not situated in this debate, and I do not understand our engagement with fictional characters as necessarily involving simulation. One of the worries about the simulationist approach to fictions is that it requires that we adopt the perspectives *of* a character,[14] but many of our thoughts and feelings towards a character's situation arise from thinking about his predicaments not through *his* eyes, but through our own. We often adopt views or have emotions about a character that the character himself would not, or even could not, share. Aristotle notes that we pity the hero of a tragedy, but the tragic hero does not pity himself. Mentalization, on the other hand, often requires that we distance ourselves from the views of a character in order to understand his situation more clearly. My discussion thus takes it for granted that we adopt a range of mental states – beliefs, desires, emotions, wishes – towards fictional characters, and that this is one of the primary reasons we read. *How* we do so lies beyond the scope of this book.

Psychoanalysis

Because I locate my discussion of mentalization and its relation to literature within a psychoanalytic view of the mind, I would like to outline the relationship between folk psychology and psychoanalysis. There has been discussion in the philosophical literature regarding whether psychoanalysis is an extension of our ordinary folk psychological way of understanding ourselves, or whether it offers a radical departure. On the face of it, there are arguments to support either position: Freud's dynamic unconscious revolutionized our understanding of the mind, and psychoanalytic concepts – from Id, Ego, and Superego to internal objects, the dynamic unconscious, the nature of phantasy, and Bion's alpha function, to name a few – are foreign to ordinary psychology. This would seem to confirm the view that psychoanalysis does something more than extend our commonsense ways of understanding ourselves, especially since psychoanalysts train many years to learn both the theory and practice of their discipline – something very different from learning folk psychology "at Granny's knee" (Fodor 1987, 6).

Is it possible both to acknowledge the Freudian revolution and yet maintain that his theory is an extension of our ordinary non-theoretical ways of thinking about ourselves? A more complete answer to this question will take us beyond the scope of this book, but let us examine some arguments in favour of this position. What is at stake is not so much an academic point that is of interest only to psychoanalytic practitioners, but rather a view on the nature of the self. Indeed, one might go further and say, quoting Socrates in *The Republic*, that, in thinking about the nature of the mind, "it is no ordinary matter that we are discussing, but the right conduct of life".[15] Psychoanalysis offers a perspective on what it means to be human that is at once both revolutionary and fundamental: revolutionary in that it not only posits mental phenomena, including a dynamic unconscious, that, until Freud, we did not have the language to grasp, but also because psychoanalysis shows us that we are ignorant – often deeply so – of our core motivations. We are regularly not the masters or mistresses of our own destinies at precisely those times in which we are convinced of the power of our agency. But as revolutionary – and upsetting – as such insights are, psychoanalysis also speaks to experiences that are all too familiar: the oldest stories of humanity are replete with heroes and heroines, villains and victims, whose actions and motivations are often hidden from them, and who deliberately act in ways that run contrary to their own flourishing. Psychoanalysis offers us new ways and insights to enable us to understand our akratic and self-deceptive behaviour. But the scope of psychoanalysis is wider than the irrational; the theory offers us a way to understand ourselves in all our humanity and complexity. Perhaps another way of putting this is to say that psychoanalysis shows us to be less rational in more ways than we previously considered either possible or desirable, but it also provides new ways of understanding ourselves, of coming to terms with the irrational elements of our nature, and it offers the means to overcome, if only in part, our self-ignorance, self-deception, and self-sabotage: where Id was, there Ego shall be.

This striving for self-understanding draws the connection between psychoanalysis and folk psychology; both are interested in understanding the self at the personal, and not the sub-personal, level. A central tenet of psychoanalysis is that our unconscious phantasies, our deepest wishes and fears, can become known to us – in part if not in whole – if we know how to examine them. Our unconscious mentality is a core – perhaps *the core* – aspect of ourselves and determines, in part, who we are in ways that are directly relevant to how we know ourselves. The aim of psychoanalytic therapy is cure by way of insight: psychoanalysis is a conversation – perhaps a rather "peculiar conversation"[16] – between two people, analyst and analysand, and therapeutic resolution is achieved by enabling the latter to gain insight into herself with the help of the former. That these insights are accessible to the analysand indicates that there is a thread – nay, a strong cord – between the insights of psychoanalysis and the understandings of folk psychology.

Freud[17] himself acknowledged the connection between psychoanalysis and folk psychology (as well as the power of great literature) by noting (in uncharacteristic humility) the shared interests of the literary writer and the scientist of the mind, and the indebtedness of the latter to the former: he notes that, given the shared interests of the fictional writer and the psychologist or psychoanalyst, it is "inevitable that science should concern herself with the same materials whose treatment by artists has given enjoyment to mankind for thousands of years, though her touch must be clumsier" (Freud 1910, 165). Psychoanalysis was, after all, developed in response to patients' suffering and was offered to them as a way both to understand the source and meaning of their symptoms, and as a cure – a "talking" cure. *Meaning* is thus central to psychoanalysis – as Freud famously wrote, "The interpretation of dreams is the royal road to a knowledge of the unconscious activities of the mind".[18] Interpretation cannot happen without the participation of the dreamer, and gaining an understanding of his symptoms was the key to cure.

Gaps in mental phenomena require explanation, and it was by positing the unconscious that Freud closed these gaps: "A gain in meaning is a perfectly justifiable ground for going beyond the limits of direct experience".[19] Positing an *unconscious* to provide meaning is necessary, says Freud: "both in healthy and in sick people psychical acts often occur which can be explained only by presupposing other acts, of which, nevertheless, consciousness affords no evidence" (Freud 1915, 166). Postulating a mental unconscious is what is known as an "inference to the best explanation"; it is the most plausible explanation available and is preferable to the alternatives, such as multiple consciousnesses or uncaused mental states. As the philosopher and psychoanalyst Jonathan Lear notes, "Psychoanalysis allows us to attribute motives where there would otherwise be gaps in the explanation of thought and behaviour – thus it is an extension of ordinary psychology".[20] By positing an unconscious, the commonsense psychological explanatory structure, whereby our beliefs and desires cause and explain our actions, remains intact – it's just that now the beliefs or the desires (or both) are unconscious. Psychoanalysis clarifies behaviour that seems inexplicable even to the agent herself, and it does so by appealing to the agent's own states of mind. Anna O[21] was pained and puzzled by her inability to quench her thirst; Freud's discovery that the cause was her repressed feeling of repulsion at observing her little dog drink from the water glass filled in the missing gaps. Once Anna O's behaviour was explicated, the symptoms vanished.[22]

Some might argue that the *kinds* of interpretations offered by psychoanalysis lie beyond the scope of ordinary explanation, disputing the connection with common-sense psychology. As Wittgenstein pointed out, modifying the term "belief" with the adjective "unconscious" changes it in a radical way – just as a "straw man" is no longer an ordinary man, so an unconscious belief is no longer an ordinary belief. The unconscious operates according to different rules – termed "primary process-ing" – from how the conscious mind operates – "secondary processing". For ex-ample, the unconscious is timeless, and mutually contradictory desires and wishes may co-exist without cancelling each other out. As Freud moved from the topo-graphic to the structural theory, the metaphor of the mind in spatial terms gave way to conceptualizing it along functional dimensions. However, although the appeal to unconscious mental states signalled new explanatory territory, the explanation still resides within the terrain of folk psychology, albeit with extended borders. So even though psychoanalysis may posit mental states and processes that are not found within folk psychology, it extends commonsense psychology rather than replaces it. The psychoanalyst Andrew Brook[23] notes that he made an inferential leap using the theory of psychoanalysis from ordinary statements that a patient made regarding her childhood. The patient had said that "even the simplest pleasures caused her to feel uneasy" (Brook 274), to which Brook responded with an interpretation regarding her superego. Brook makes the point that not only does psychoanalysis extend com-monsense psychology, but "clinical practice depends on [it]" (Brook 275).

But dependency is not enough to show that psychoanalysis is an extension of folk psychology, because one theory may depend on another even as it departs radi-cally from it. Psychoanalysis, though, retains and develops core elements of folk psychology in "establishing and maintaining the intersubjective, communicative field between analyst and analysand" (Brook p 278). It is this shared subjectiv-ity in the enterprise of finding meaning that most deeply connects psychoanalysis with folk psychology. Compare a psychoanalytic explanation of behaviour with one from, say, neuroscience: a patient is told she is depressed because her sero-tonin levels are too low. As noted earlier, this kind of explanation is no longer about finding meaning but about positing causes, and the patient as agent is re-moved from the picture: "essential to psychoanalysis is the view that the process of self-understanding, of insight, of coming to know oneself or even of attempting to do so, is the kind of satisfaction that psychoanalytic practice has to offer".[24]

Mentalization

The previous discussion has stressed the centrality of features such as intention-ality, perspective, narrative, and understanding as core to both commonsense psychology and psychoanalysis. They both provide explanations of human behaviour at the personal level by shining light on the beliefs, desires, wishes, and intentions that both motivate and explain behaviour. Recent work in developmental psychoanalysis has provided a useful concept that enables us to home in on these central features. The key concept is that of mentalization.

Mentalization was first introduced in psychoanalysis in the 1960s by the French psychoanalysts Pierre Marty and Pierre Luquet;[25] the term and its related verb *mentalizing* were developed further and introduced into the contemporary psychological literature by Peter Fonagy, György Gergely, Elliot Jurist, and Mary Target.[26] The term refers to the specific abilities required to understand ourselves and those around us and to predict their behaviour. Mentalization involves reflecting on the nature of ourselves as thinking, feeling beings, and understanding that our cognitive and emotional capacities are not just characteristics of who we are, but central to how we navigate the world and negotiate with others. In the words of Fonagy et al., "Mentalization . . . is the process by which we realize that having a mind mediates our experience of the world" (Fonagy et al. 2002, 3). Mentalization is a developmental achievement – not only in the empirical sense that our mental and emotional capacities develop as we grow, but also in the sense that mentalizing is an activity that characterizes mature mental functioning. Individuals with various personality or psychological disorders may struggle to mentalize, and mentalization-based therapy has found to be highly effective in treating patients with borderline personality disorder,[27] for example. But impairments to mentalization may occur in otherwise well-functioning individuals too: during times of stress or distress, our ability to think carefully about or understand our own or others' motivations may be compromised. Fonagy et al. emphasize that an important aspect of mentalization is the regulation of affect. Mentalization involves thinking not only about thinking, but about feelings and emotions. Mentalization impacts a person's ability to manage her emotional states. Mentalized affectivity "marks a mature capacity for the regulation of affect and denotes the capacity to discover the subjective meanings of one's own affect states" (Fonagy et al. 5). Elliot Jurist[28] points out that "we do not always know what we feel" (Jurist 2005, 429), and the ability to fathom the implications of our own and others' emotional lives often "requires a process of working through the manifestations of our representational world in current affective experience" (429). He claims[29] that mentalized affectivity "fosters a new, more differentiated kind of affect and self-regulation" (Jurist 2010, 291), which entails "revaluing, not just modulating, affects" (297). Such revaluation may lead to creating new meaning regarding past events so as to enable us to possess "a more profound sense of living in the present" (297).

The psychoanalyst Jeremy Holmes[30] usefully delineates four interrelated aspects of mentalization capacities: (1) mentalizing is a metacognitive phenomenon that involves "thinking about thinking", which is (2) "concerned with the *meanings* which we attribute to our own and others' actions" (Holmes 2005, 180, italics in original) – it is key to how we understand one another by attributing motives, conscious or unconscious, that allows us to make sense of behaviour. Mentalization is also (3) central to how we respond to another as a *person*, and thus it is an important constituent of personhood; and (4) "Mentalizing is not a fixed property of mind, but is a *process*, a capacity, or skill, which may be present or absent to a greater or lesser degree" (Holmes 2005, 180, italics in original). Mentalization involves a flexible state of mind and marks an ability to "alter one's judgment in the light of new information and the complexity of the phenomena, and attention to coherence, qualification, and nuance in one's judgments of motives".[31] Mentalizing involves an ability to think about both one's own inner life and the inner lives of others; it indicates the capacity for flexibility in judgement and an ability to distinguish between fantasy and reality. Mature mentalizing capacities also enable one to distinguish one's empathic understanding of another from one's projections onto others – a key element in the recognition of other states of mind. Knowing what belongs to me enables me to know whether I am misreading your states of mind, or whether I am picking up on cues that accurately reflect what is going on for you.

There is some discussion in the literature[32] about whether the term "mentalization" adds something new to psychology or whether it is old wine in new bottles. Since it focuses more on the capacities to understand oneself and others than on, say, the dynamics of unconscious mental functioning, is it a theory that falls within psychoanalysis? Fonagy et al. certainly think so, and they claim that mentalized affectivity lies "at the core of the psychotherapeutic enterprise" (Fonagy et al. 2002, 5). The term captures more than a "thin" ability to engage in mind reading and includes the capacity to distinguish between inner and outer reality; the ability to engage in "pretend play", which requires an ability to think abstractly; and a capacity for insight and self-reflection. To quote Fonagy et al. (2002) again: "mentalization is a concept with a rich history in both psychoanalytic theory . . . and cognitive psychology" (3). To put this another way: if we understand mentalization from a psychoanalytic perspective such that the term carries with it a concept of the mind that is imbued with the characteristics central to psychoanalysis (internal objects, a dynamic unconscious, mature and immature defence mechanisms, primary and secondary processing, and so on), we will understand that the ability to mentalize includes more than a commonsense psychological understanding of knowing one's own mind and interpreting the behaviour of others. Mentalizing, understood from within a psychoanalytic picture of the mind, means that a person is able to distinguish the mental states of others from her own projections. She will be less likely to resort to immature defence mechanisms (splitting, projecting), and she will be able to regulate affect and refrain from "acting out" in times of stress. A person who mentalizes successfully is adept at distinguishing between phantasy and reality, between her internal world and the psychologies of others. The psychoanalyst Mary Target[33] agrees and argues that mentalization is part of psychoanalysis broadly understood.

The theory of stages of mentalization underlying the development of personality and relatedness . . . is psychoanalytic in that it concerns the unconscious foundations of mental functioning, which may be dynamically as well as descriptively unconscious.

(Target 2007, 262)

Mentalization, in both its theoretical origins and clinical use, is steeped in ways of understanding ourselves that are fundamentally psychoanalytic. Mentalization is clearly compatible with some other theories of "mind reading", but there are also important differences. Discussions about theory of mind in cognitive science tend to refer mainly to mental states involving propositional attitudes – beliefs and desires – without locating this discussion in a personal-level psychological theory, and certainly not in a theory that makes space for a dynamic unconscious. Because mentalization stresses the centrality of affect and emotion in ways that require not only understanding but re-evaluation, mentalization and mentalized affectivity is psychoanalytic at heart.

It is thus through the lens of psychoanalysis that mentalization and mentalizing abilities are understood in the discussions to follow. By highlighting the ways in which mentalization can assist in understanding other psychological factors, the case for the importance of mentalization as offering significant insights regarding our psychological lives will be strengthened. For example, a psychoanalytic understanding of mentalization enables us to understand the role that different kinds of defence mechanisms play in enabling or hindering mentalizing capabilities. Rigid defence mechanisms are as much a bar to mentalization as defences overwhelmed by unconscious phantasy. A person who thinks along mental paths that are unyielding and repetitive may fail at certain aspects of mentalization as much as someone whose thoughts are scattered and uncontained. We can further understand mentalization via Freud's distinction between primary and secondary processing – mentalization would be influenced less by primary modes of thinking dominated by unconscious phantasy and irrational defensive strategies, and more by secondary processing governed by rationality and responsiveness to reality. An unconscious attunement to another would not necessarily indicate good mentalizing capacities. What would be required are higher-order cognitive attitudes that can reflect on the nature of that attunement and think about what it means: whether it is appropriate or inappropriate, an accurate perception or an inappropriate projection, and so on. Mentalization is also to be distinguished from empathy, if we understand the latter term to mean something like "feeling an emotion with someone, and because the other is feeling it".[34] For example, if Phoebe empathizes with Kobi about the loss of his favourite toy, she will feel sad because she knows that Kobi feels sad. But such empathic sadness does not necessarily involve mentalization: Phoebe may be very sensitive and highly attuned to Kobi, but she may not understand that she is sad *because* Kobi is feeling sad. Mentalization involves that extra step – the ability to reflect on one's sadness so that one understands why one is feeling a particular way. Mentalization is not emotional contagion. Indeed, the ability to mentalize may often prevent one from feeling *with* another: Phoebe may feel sad *for* Kobi because he mourns his favourite toy without sharing his sadness. She may understand that Kobi feels sad without feeling sad herself. The ability to mentalize requires the ability to distinguish one's own emotional and cognitive states from those of another, so that even when one feels an emotion in response to someone else, one will not confuse one's own thoughts or feelings with those of the other person.

Mentalization and Literature

The focus in the chapters that follow is on the ways in which literary form – or at least some kinds of literary form – enable mentalization. The selection of texts and literary devices are of necessity cherry-picked; it would be a gargantuan task to analyse all the different kinds and ways in which literary form enables mentalization. When I say that literary form "enables" mentalization, I am not making the empirical claim that reading literature, or good literature, teaches us how to mentalize. Although there is empirical evidence to suggest that this is indeed the case,[35] it is also highly likely that the skills required to be alive to the nuances of a Jane Austen novel or a Miltonic sonnet *require* a well-developed ability to mentalize. My suggestion is not that reading good literature creates our ability to mentalize, especially as adults; reading any kind of fiction, from popular romance novels to paperback thrillers, requires an ability to mentalize, as it would be otherwise impossible to understand characters' inner lives, motivations, and action. Literary fiction will at least involve such mind-reading capacities, but it also enhances it. We learn ways of understanding our emotions and our mind-reading skills via formal literary techniques, especially those techniques in the hands of a gifted author. We read the great novelists and poets not only for plot or content, but for insight. Socrates criticized[36] the representational arts for doing little more than holding up a mirror to nature; but, as the art critic and philosopher Arthur Danto[37] points out, mirrors reflect not only the external world, but also ourselves too.

Although there have been many works on psychoanalysis and art and creativity, from Freud[38] to Ernest Jones,[39] Marion Milner,[40] Hanna Segal,[41] and so on, the focus is either on the *content* of the work or on the use of literature as an example of a psychoanalytic issue or idea, such as the torment of Hamlet as an illustration of an unresolved Oedipus complex. The discussion here focuses less on the relationship between literature and unconscious phantasy and more on the ways in which literature can sharpen our metacognitive and meta-affective abilities. I do not deny the importance of unconscious phantasy, of course; nor do I deny that literature may provide important insights into the nature of the human condition. The conversation between writers and psychoanalysts, between the literary and the psychoanalytic, is likely to be as various and complex as human nature itself. The emphasis on mentalization is a shift of focus, not a denial of the relevance of other aspects of psychoanalysis to literature, or indeed of literature to psychoanalysis.

Perspective

One focus in the chapters that follow – specifically in the discussion on Jane Austen – will be the role of *perspective-taking*. The ability to mentalize requires, in part, a capacity to take on or adopt the perspective of another whilst maintaining one's own sense of identity. On this account, empathy or sympathy does not imply the merging of identities; indeed, as noted earlier, such merging is incompatible with mentalization. Thinking about the mind of another often requires that we consider her situation from various perspectives – from her own, through the eyes of another, or from the viewpoint of an omniscient narrator. We may, following David Hume and Wayne C. Booth,[42] view the narrator himself as a literary character through whose perspective we understand the lives of the characters. In his famous essay "Of the Standard of Taste",[43] Hume notes that we "choose our favourite author as we do our friend, from a conformity of humour and disposition" (244) – so much so, in fact, that Hume thinks we cannot adopt the perspective of an author whose sympathies we cannot endorse, or whose ethical or moral values we abjure. Booth also argues for approaching literature via the metaphor of befriending the author:

> when I read *Don Quixote, Persuasion, Bleak House*, or *War and Peace*, I meet in their authors friends who demonstrate their friendship . . . in the irresistible invitation they extend to live during these moments a richer and fuller life than I could manage on my own.
>
> (Booth 1988, 223)

If this is so, then reading almost *any* novel requires mentalizing skills, as we are asked to adopt or question, in the case of an unreliable narrator, the author's perspective. Reading good literature is not merely a cognitive skill, but a normative exercise: it engages our sympathies and understanding in exactly the same kinds of ways that our engagement with others requires.

Stream-of-Consciousness

Note that some literary techniques that may seem at first glance to require or reflect good mentalizing skills or capacities may in fact not do so. Stream-of-consciousness, for example, provides an immediate access to the mind of a character and may seem a good candidate as an example of a literary technique that facilitates mentalizing skills. It was developed partly in response to psychoanalytic discoveries about the mind, which, claims David Lodge,[44] "encouraged the idea that consciousness had a dimension of depth, which it was the task of literature, as of psychoanalysis, to explore" (Lodge 2002, 61). One of the novelists who experimented with this technique was Virginia Woolf.[45] Here is an excerpt from *Mrs Dalloway*:

> For it was the middle of June. The War was over, except for someone like Mrs. Foxcroft at the Embassy last night eating her heart out because that nice boy was killed and now the old Manor House must go to a cousin; or Lady Bexborough who opened a bazaar, they said, with the telegram in her hand, John, her favourite, killed; but it was over; thank Heaven – over. It was June. The King and Queen were at the Palace. And everywhere, though it was still so early, there was a beating, a stirring of galloping ponies, tapping of cricket bats.
>
> (Woolf 2013, 2)

Here we gain immediate access into the mind of Mrs Dalloway; we see, hear, and feel through her consciousness. There is an interweaving of past and present as her mind flits from thought to thought, which are a mix of imagined sights and sounds. Overheard or remembered bits of news or gossip mingle with her concerns about the war and her hopes for the future. We feel her joy about the ending of the war; we hear the tap of cricket ball against bat, and see in our mind's eye the galloping ponies as she projects into their movement her own renewed enthusiasm for life. Stream-of-consciousness presents us with immediate access to her mind. The rhythm and cadence of the language mirrors the rhythm and cadence of Mrs Dalloway's thought patterns, and Woolf's imagery does the dual work of allowing us to look through her mental states, and at them, simultaneously. The descriptions capture the qualities of the scenes experienced or imagined as well as Mrs Dalloway's responses to these scenes. The effect of Woolf's writing is to stimulate in the reader a shared sense of Mrs Dalloway's state of mind – our thought patterns adjust to the tempo and rhythm of the lines as we read.

Stream-of-consciousness as a literary technique does not necessarily facilitate our mentalizing abilities; we see the world through the eyes of the characters and adopt a perspective on their consciousness. However, and perhaps somewhat counter-intuitively, the immediacy of this style may present a barrier to mentalization. If a key component of mentalization is the ability to adopt a higher-order perspective, to take a step back and consider the nature of another's ideas or emotions and our responses to them, then stream-of-consciousness may sometimes dim mentalization rather than sharpen it. This is especially so when the reader is asked to adopt the perspective of a character whose self-knowledge is limited. Neither sympathy nor empathy is sufficient for mentalization; what is required is an ability to differentiate one's own mental states from that of another, to adopt a meta-perspective that does not elide the barriers between self and other. Another example that illustrates this point is the "Penelope" episode of *Ulysses*,[46] in which James Joyce captures the unconscious chain of associations that lead Molly Bloom from thought to thought:

> I suppose he was glad to get shut of her and her dog smelling my fur and always edging to get up under my petticoats especially then still I like that in him polite to old women like that and waiters and beggars too hes not proud out of nothing but not always if ever he got anything really serious the matter with him its much better for them go into a hospital where everything is clean but I suppose Id have to dring it into him for a month yes.
>
> (Joyce 1986 [1922], 608)

Molly's thoughts meander from one idea to the next, and the reader struggles to reconstruct the development of her thinking. There is something dreamlike about her ruminations, reflected too in the use of run-on lines; it is difficult to know when a sentence or thought begins and ends. Syntactic structure is necessary for sense and sense-making. Molly's lack of insight into her own motivations also makes it difficult for the reader to gain clarity regarding what she is thinking and feeling.

The stream-of-consciousness technique may derail efforts to mentalize about the minds of the characters precisely because of the very immediate way their thoughts are presented to the reader. The ability to think *about* someone else's state of mind requires psychical distance, which stream-of-consciousness attempts to collapse.

Literature as Humanistic Endeavour

If engaging with the narrator of a novel is akin to our engagement with the mind of another, this goes some way towards explaining the lure and allure of literature – in reading, we engage someone else's thoughts and feel that we are not alone. We also treat characters as persons, with beliefs, desires, emotion, and complex inner worlds, and with whom we empathize, sympathize, and criticize. Literature triggers our mentalization abilities – and good literature, I suggest, helps develop them via narrative techniques that facilitate the reader's capacity for mentalization. My discussion of literature is that it is at heart a humanistic endeavour, which includes the claims[47] not only that literary works "bear on the world" and "have cognitive value" (Gaskin 2016, 63) but more importantly that literature is concerned with the fundamental questions of what it means to be human. It is not only philosophy that is concerned with how to live, and it is not only tragedy, as Aristotle noted, that is like philosophy. Literature, in the words of Bernard Harrison,[48] "is concerned with words not as things in themselves, but as signs and tools of the multifarious practices by means of which we continually recreate ourselves" (271). This book can be read, although that is not its explicit argument, as part of that defence of literature. Literature employs narrative for the same kinds of reasons that commonsense psychology employs narrative: to bring to light the hidden springs and wells that irrigate and sustain human activity.

Notes

1 Aristotle, *Poetics*, trans. S.H. Butcher (Macmillan, 1895), Chapter VI.
2 E.M. Forster, *Aspects of the Novel* (Hodder & Stoughton, 2016 [1905]), Chapter 5, eBook.
3 Deborah Knight, "A Poetics of Psychological Explanation", *Metaphilosophy* 28, nos. 1 & 2 (1997): 63–80.
4 Donald Davidson, "Mental Events", in *Essays on Actions and Events* (Oxford University Press, 2001): 170–187.
5 Donald Davidson, "Psychology as Philosophy", in *Essays on Actions and Events* (Oxford University Press, 2001): 191.
6 Jerry A. Fodor, "The Persistence of the Attitudes", in *Psychosemantics* (MIT Press, 1987): 3.
7 Daniel Dennett, *Content and Consciousness* (Routledge, 1969): 164
8 See for example Paul Churchland, "Eliminative Materialism and the Propositional Attitudes", *Journal of Philosophy* 78 (1981): 67–90; Steve Stich, *Deconstructing the Mind* (Oxford University Press, 1996).
9 Alison Gopnik and Henry M. Wellman, "Why the Child's Theory of Mind Really Is a Theory", *Mind & Language* 7, nos. 1 & 2 (1992): 145–171.

10 The false belief test is discussed, *inter alia*, in Alan Leslie, "Pretense and Representation: The Origins of 'Theory of Mind'", *Psychological Review* 94, no. 4 (1987): 412–426; Steve Stich and Shaun Nichols, "Folk Psychology: Simulation or Tacit Theory?", *Mind & Language* 7, no. 1 (1992): 35–71; and Heinz Wimmer and Josef Perner, "Beliefs about Beliefs: Representation and Constraining Function of Wrong Beliefs in Young Children's Understanding of Deception", *Cognition* 13 (1983): 103–128.

11 The claim that having a belief requires that we also have a concept of belief raises important questions about whether, say, other animals have beliefs. I do not rule out the possibility that other animals have beliefs, but if they do, they will be different in kind from the kinds of beliefs that persons have. Whether these differences are differences of kind or degree is a discussion that takes us beyond the scope of this book.

12 Colin Radford and Michael Weston, "How Can We Be Moved by the Fate of Anna Karenina?", *Proceedings of the Aristotelian Society, Supplementary* 49 (1975): 67–93.

13 Arthur Conan Doyle, "The Musgrave Ritual", in *The Memoirs of Sherlock Holmes* (Ballantine Books, 1975): 86–106.

14 Wollheim's notion of "central imagining", to be discussed in Chapters 2 and 5.

15 Plato, "The Republic", in *Plato: The Collected Dialogues*, eds. and trans. Edith Hamilton and Huntington Cairns (Princeton University Press, 1961): 603 (352d).

16 Jonathan Lear, *Freud* (Routledge, 2005).

17 Sigmund Freud, "A Special Type of Choice of Object Made by Men", in *The Standard Edition of the Complete Psychological Works of Sigmund Freud (Henceforth SE) XI*, ed. and trans. James Strachey (Hogarth Press, 1910): 163–175.

18 Sigmund Freud, *The Interpretation of Dreams* SE IV (1900): 608.

19 Sigmund Freud, *The Unconscious* SE XIV (1915): 167.

20 Jonathan Lear, "The Heterogeneity of the Mental", *Mind* 104, no. 416 (1995): 863–879.

21 Sigmund Freud and Josef Breuer, "Studies on Hysteria", in *SE* II, ed. and trans. James Strachey (Hogarth Press, 1895): 1–305.

22 The relationship between interpretation and cure is obviously far more complicated and circuitous than this account would have us believe; nevertheless, for my purposes here, I'll accept that it is very roughly descriptively accurate.

23 Andrew Brook, "Psychoanalysis and Commonsense Psychology", *The Annual of Psychoanalysis* 20 (1992): 273–303.

24 Rachel Blass and Zvi Carmeli, "The Case against Neuropsychoanalysis", *International Journal of Psychoanalysis* 88 (2007): 19–40, at 37.

25 See the discussion in Catherine Freeman, "What Is Mentalizing? An Overview", *British Journal of Psychotherapy* 32, no. 2 (2016): 189–201.

26 Peter Fonagy, Mary Target, Gyorgy Gergely, and Elliot L. Jurist, *Affect Regulation, Mentalization and the Development of the Self* (Routledge, 2002)

27 See, for example, Anthony Bateman and Peter Fonagy, *Psychotherapy for Borderline Personality Disorder: Mentalization Based Treatment* (Oxford University Press, 2004); Anthony Bateman and Peter Fonagy, "Comorbid Antisocial and Borderline Personality Disorders: Mentalization-Based Treatment", *Journal of Clinical Psychology: In Session* 64, no. 2 (2008): 181–194.

28 Elliot L. Jurist, "Mentalized Affectivity", *Psychoanalytic Psychology* 22, no. 3 (2005): 426–444.

29 Elliot L. Jurist, "Mentalizing Minds", *Psychoanalytic Inquiry* 30, no. 4 (2010): 289–300.

30 Jeremy Holmes, "Notes on Mentalizing – Old Hat, or New Wine?", *British Journal of Psychotherapy* 22, no. 2 (2005): 179–197.

31 Michael Lacewing, "Psychodynamic Psychotherapy, Insight and Therapeutic Action", *Clinical Psychology: Science and Practice* 21, no. 2 (2014): 154–171.

32 Jeremy Holmes, "Notes on Mentalizing – Old Hat, or New Wine?", *British Journal of Psychotherapy* 22, no. 2 (2005): 179–197.

33 Mary Target, "Commentary," in *Mentalization: Theoretical Considerations, Research Findings, and Clinical Implications*, ed. Fredric N. Busch (The Analytic Press, 2008): 261–279. See also Peter Fonagy and Mary Target, "The Rooting of the Mind in the Body: New Links between Attachment Theory and Psychoanalytic Thought", *Journal of the American Psychoanalytic Association* 55 (2007): 411–456.

34 Nancy Snow, "Empathy", *American Philosophical Quarterly* 37, no. 1 (200): 65–78, at 66.

35 See, for example, Melissa Chapple, Philip Davis, Josie Billington, Sophie Williams, and Rhiannon Corcoran, "Challenging Empathic Deficit Models of Autism through Responses to Serious Literature", *Frontiers in Psychology* 13 (2022): 1–15; David Comer Kidd and Emanuele Castano, "Reading Literary Fiction Improves Theory of Mind", *Science* 342, no. 6156 (2013): 377–380.

36 Plato, "The Republic," in *Plato: The Collected Dialogues*, eds. and trans. Edith Hamilton and Huntington Cairns (Princeton University Press, 1961): 821 (596d–e).

37 Arthur Danto, "Works of Art and Mere Real Things", in *The Transfiguration of the Commonplace* (Harvard University Press, 1981).

38 Sigmund Freud, "Creative Writers and Day Dreaming", in *The Standard Edition of the Complete Psychological Works of Sigmund Freud (SE)*, Volume 9, ed. and trans. James Strachey (Hogarth Press, 1907): 141–154.

39 Ernst Jones, *"The Problem of Hamlet and the Oedipus-Complex" – an Introductory Essay to Shakespeare's Hamlet* (Vision Press, 1947).

40 Marion Milner, *On Not Being Able to Paint* (Routledge, 2010).

41 Hanna Segal, "A Psycho-Analytic Approach to Aesthetics", *The International Journal of Psychoanalysis* 33 (1952): 196–207.

42 Wayne C. Booth, *The Company We Keep* (University of California Press, 1988).

43 David Hume, "Of the Standard of Taste," in *Essays: Moral, Political and Literary*, ed. Eugene F. Miller (Indianapolis: Liberty Classics, 1987 [1757]): 226–249.

44 David Lodge, *Consciousness and the Novel* (Harvard University Press, 2002).

45 Virginia Woolf, *Mrs Dalloway* (HarperCollins, 2013 [1925]).

46 James Joyce, *Ulysses* (Vintage, 1986 [1922]).

47 Richard Gaskin, *Language, Truth and Literature* (Oxford University Press, 2016).

48 Bernard Harrison, *What Is Fiction For?* (Indiana University Press, 2014).

Chapter 2

Form

Form matters. In aesthetics, form is understood as "an essential shaping principle".[1] Aristotle contrasted form with matter; the latter provides the material out of which a work of art is created, and the form shapes that material. A sculpture of a bird can be made from a variety of material; it can be cast in bronze, carved from wood, or sculpted in marble. Form in literature is conceptual or abstract rather than concrete: how a novel or play or poem is written – its length, structure, the relation between incidents, rhyme scheme, point of view, and so on – organizes its content. Narrative content is the story – what the novel or poem is about – while the form presents this content to the reader in a particular way. Knowing the form of a piece may tell us how to approach a literary work: lovers of detective fiction anticipate that the crime will be solved by the detective, who is (usually) not the same person as the criminal; romantic novels end with a love match. Tragedy, as Aristotle points out, gives rise to feelings of pity and fear. Content matters too, of course: a tragedy must involve the demise of a virtuous person and not a criminal, and the tragic hero must come to an understanding of his actions by the end of the play.

In the best works, form and content work seamlessly together. But the role of form is essential and primes an audience's expectations. An artist may surprise us if these expectations are subverted: one of the reasons the movie *Psycho* was so upsetting to viewers is that the heroine, played by a well-known actress, was murdered near the beginning of the film. Hitchcock subverted the conventions of the suspense thriller to discomfort the audience. Agatha Christie caused a great deal of consternation with the publication of *The Murder of Roger Ackroyd*, which deliberately exploited the traditional murder mystery genre to deceive the reader. This is not to deny that classifying literature along formal criteria is often tricky: writes Northrop Frye,[2]

> In novels that we think of as typical, like those of Jane Austen, plot and dialogue are closely linked to the conventions of the comedy of manners. The conventions of *Wuthering Heights* are linked rather with the tale and the ballad.
>
> (Frye 1950, 583)

DOI: 10.4324/9781032702278-3

Frye's point is that formal conventions are not prescriptive rules, and a piece of writing may contain elements that are consistent with other literary genres, while one work of a genre may contain elements that would be disruptive for other works of the same genre. In short, giving necessary and sufficient conditions for literary form, even within genres, is more rule of thumb than science. As Hume[3] notes,

> To check the sallies of the imagination, and to reduce every expression to geometrical truth and exactness, would be the most contrary to the laws of criticism; because it would produce a work, which, by universal experience, has been found the most insipid and disagreeable.
>
> (Hume 1987 [1757], 231)

Nevertheless, form is essential to art: its relation to content can be analogized as syntax to semantics. Form enables content to be portrayed, apprehended, and comprehended.

As noted in the previous chapter, the difference between plot and story is one of form: a story tells of incidents, but a plot relates them via a particular order and structure. Form shapes our thoughts: we are *informed* because the *what* of a story is presented to us in a particular way and from a particular perspective. *How* we think structures *what* we think, and even *that* we think: if we understand Bion's notion of a container as that function (termed by him the "alpha function") which transforms inchoate representations into thoughts with representational content, then formal elements are crucial for the creation of thought itself. Form also shapes our emotional expectations: we expect a limerick to be funny, a haiku to present compact wisdom or insight, and a sonnet to be lyrical. Our expectations may be thwarted, sometimes deliberately, but the formal styles of these different genres of poetry are important in shaping them. This is the case with all forms of literature; a writer may abide by the conventions of a genre or subvert them, but form plays an essential role in art.

Kant

One of the most influential philosophers to discuss the importance of form was Immanuel Kant,[4] whose emphasis on the importance of form for our appreciation of the aesthetic influenced the formalist movement of the 1920s, which includes well-known artists and art critics such as Clive Bell and Roger Fry. In his *Critique of Judgement*, Kant gives an account of the aesthetic experience, with particular focus on the experience of the beautiful, on the one hand, and the sublime, on the other. Form plays a significant part of the account. Our experience of the beautiful, which is essentially pleasurable and harmonious, is shaped by form, while the sublime, which inspires awe, fear, and a sense of being overwhelmed, is characterized by formlessness. The harmony and symmetry of form prevents the mind from being overwhelmed by its experiences.

Form is also important for Kant because it ensures the universal nature of our experience: what distinguishes the experience of the beautiful from what Kant calls "the agreeable" is that the former does not depend on any specific individual taste or situation – we take pleasure in a beautiful object in virtue of our shared humanity. My enjoyment of the richness of a chocolate ganache is an instance of the agreeable: not everyone shares my taste, but the beauty of Monet's painting *The Water Lily Pond* is a joy that anyone who views the painting can and indeed ought to experience. Of course, the viewer must adopt the appropriate state of mind – the appreciation of beauty requires focused contemplation. The pleasure we take in the beautiful is not limited to this or that person, but is available to everyone. The role that form plays in the universalizability of the aesthetic experience is fundamental, and it is linked to the role of the Faculty of the Understanding or Reason. Prior to Kant, the Scottish philosopher Francis Hutcheson[5] claimed that objects were beautiful insofar as they exhibited "uniformity amidst variety" – regularity and complexity. Hutcheson wanted to provide a mathematical-type account of the nature of beauty which acknowledged the importance of strict form, although as later philosophers[6] noted, it is impossible to characterize beautiful or aesthetically pleasing objects via a formula. However, Hutcheson's account importantly recognized the centrality of form.

Reason and Imagination

For Kant, our rational faculties play a crucial role in our experience of the beautiful – unlike the agreeable, which is exhausted by physical sensation. The experience of the beautiful – what Kant calls a "judgement of taste" – involves a harmonious free play of the cognitive faculties of the imagination and understanding. The imagination is that faculty which organizes the data of sense experience, but it does not provide us with knowledge. The ways in which the imagination presents experiences to us are imprecise: as Descartes[7] famously noted, we cannot *imagine* with any precision what a chiliagon looks like, although we can *understand* with our rational faculty that it is a polygon of a thousand sides. The mental faculty that makes knowledge possible is the Understanding, which organizes sense experience via concepts. It is because we have concepts that we can cognize the world around us. We categorize the natural world, for example, into trees and flowers and fruits, and more finely into elm trees, pines, and oaks. Without such concepts, we could not make sense of the phenomena of experience. Concepts, which are the formal mental capacities for understanding the world around us, are sense-making. The external world provides the content, which our minds organize into a coherent experience. As Kant famously says in his *Critique of Pure Reason*, "Thoughts without content are empty, intuitions without concepts are blind".[8] Concepts provide shape and form, but not content, which is why Kant claims they are "empty"; like cookie cutters, they mould the dough of experience into recognizable figures. The beautiful is experienced as "purposiveness without purpose", in which all the parts seem to strive towards a single end but without any actual purpose that would go beyond the experience itself. However, because our experience of beauty gives rise to pleasure and not knowledge, the concepts of the understanding do not organize experience in rigid conformity to our concepts; rather, as noted earlier, Kant stresses that there is a "free play" between the imagination and the understanding – our rational faculties are responsible for organizing and containing our experience, but the playfulness of the imagination – the non-formal elements, if you will – play a crucial role too.

For Kant, form explains why the aesthetic experience is a universal one; it gives credence to the classical tradition's emphasis on regularity and harmony in art, and it makes the case for form as necessary for the harmonious experience of the beautiful. According to Kant, the experience of beauty is quintessentially one of *internal harmony*; this is contrasted with his account of the sublime, which is experienced as formless, uncontained, and hence overwhelming. Kant's contribution to aesthetics also alerts us to the importance of the rational faculties: contemplation is made possible only when the mind is not overwhelmed by impressions, but when it can take a step back and reflect on what it apprehends. It is Kant's contribution to the *reflective* and *contemplative* aspects of the aesthetic experience that this book emphasizes – not all aspects of his account will be relevant for our purposes. For instance, Kant famously derides the lures of charm and other emotions which arise from non-formal elements in an artwork. For Kant, form gives rise to an *aesthetic* emotion, a rarified state of mind that is distinct from our ordinary "garden variety" emotions. One of the claims of this book is that works of art – specifically works of literature – *do* engage with our ordinary emotional lives in ways which are rich and rewarding. Form orders and directs our attention and provides the necessary structure to enable us to focus, organize, and comprehend our experiences. This is crucial for another important feature of formal properties – their role in containing and modifying difficult emotions. One of the functions of form is as a container for strong emotions. Aristotle's insistence that a good tragedy be constructed in a particular way – *plot is the soul of tragedy* – is an example of the ways in which form, understood as structure, is necessary lest the tragic emotions of pity and fear overwhelm the audience and prevent them from achieving the insight necessary to achieve *katharsis*, the aesthetic pleasure unique to classical tragedy, according to Aristotle. The psychoanalyst Hanna Segal develops an account of tragic pleasure that takes its cue from Aristotle, and she too acknowledges the importance of form for aesthetics. Before I discuss Segal's views, I shall outline some of the key psychoanalytic concepts that play a central part of her account.

Paranoid-Schizoid and Depressive Positions

Segal was an analysand of Melanie Klein, and her most well-known follower and interpreter. She made Klein's often dense prose available to a wider audience and applied Klein's thought to many disciplines, including social and political commentary, and aesthetics. Klein's contributions to psychoanalysis cannot be understated.

She changed the emphasis in psychoanalysis from Freud's focus on the phases of libidinal development to a theory of object relations. Klein argued that our internal worlds are constituted by internal objects, first modelled on the infant's relationship with his parents, although "internal objects are not exact replicas of real external objects, but are always coloured by the infant's phantasy and projections".[9]

Klein also described two major stages involved in psychological development. The first stage, known as the Paranoid-Schizoid position (P/S for short), is characterized by an internal world that is fractured: emotions are undifferentiated, as is the relationship between the self and the external world. The baby is unable to distinguish himself from his mother: as Winnicott famously stated, "there is no such thing as an infant"[10] because the distinction between self and (m)other is not well delineated. During the P/S phase, the infant's world consists of internal objects whose nature is defined by the infant's experiences: the mother who feeds and cares for the infant is experienced as a "good mother", while the mother who is experienced as withholding food or care is the "bad mother". Because the identity of the mother is wholly determined by the infant's affects or feelings, "good mother" and "bad mother" are experienced not as aspects of the same person, but as different mothers. These maternal figures constitute Klein's notion of "internal objects": they are felt to reside within the mind of the infant and are constitutive of his inner world. Internal objects are "part objects" – the "good mother" or "bad mother" represents only an aspect of the mother who is internalized but, as noted by Laplanche and Pontalis,[11] internal objects are "phantastically endowed with powers analogous to those of a person" (Laplanche and Pontalis 1988, 188). In order to defend himself against the bad object, the infant will resort to using whatever defence mechanisms are at his disposal; these usually consist in expelling (projecting) from the self the bad objects and holding onto or identifying with the good objects. Such defence mechanisms operate at the level of phantasy, where the mind conceives of itself in bodily terms.

During the P/S phase, the infant is unable to think: its world is dominated by these part-objects that are acted upon via primitive defence mechanisms. Freud referred to this as "primary process thinking", while Bion devised the term "beta function" to describe the mental operations that are dominant during this phase. Symington and Symington note that the beta function acts upon beta particles, which are fragmented[12] "sense impressions devoid of meaning or nameless sensations which cause frustration" (Symington and Symington, 2002: 62). Beta elements are experienced, not as thoughts with propositional content, but as bits of the body or bodily functions. Via these concepts, Bion is trying to capture the inchoate nature of the mind at this time.

The P/S position or phase contrasts with what Klein terms the "depressive position", which marks the move from an inchoate merged experience with the mother to a newly emerging self. In the depressive position, the baby realizes that "hated-mother" and "loved-mother" are not two different mothers, but two *aspects* of the same mother. In attacking the "bad mother", the infant has also damaged the "good mother". This gives rise to feelings of guilt, and the infant is now moved to repair the attacks against the mother. This is the germ of reparation. It is important to bear in mind that via the act of reparation, the infant is also forming his own thinking mind. Reparative activity replaces the split-off internal objects with whole objects, which are experienced not as endowed with powers of a person, but rather as internal representations of a mother who resides outside the self. Reparation allows for the growth of the self as it separates from the external world, and the infant learns to situate his or her place in that world. It is also during the depressive position that the infant begins to develop a thinking mind.

Reparative activity is the key to mental functioning. It is during the emergence of the depressive position that thinking develops. Thinking requires an ability to see logical connections between propositions; it requires a level of abstraction such that we can distinguish between a word and what it represents. Thinkers engage in a kind of "free play": we can substitute a word with its synonym, and the sentence retains its meaning. This is a developmental achievement and stands in contrast to the P/S position, where words are not clearly distinguished from what they represent. This kind of P/S thinking is operative in magical thinking, for example, where words are experienced as having the force of physical objects: to cast a spell on someone or to curse them is to think of language as having the power to act directly on phenomena in the external world. In the depressive position, on the other hand, we can freely associate between ideas, noting non-logical connections that give rise to imaginary scenarios. Such thinking is governed by Freud's "secondary processing" and is enabled by Bion's "alpha function". The alpha function "acts on the data from a person's total emotional experience" and "renders this emotional experience comprehensible and meaningful, by producing alpha elements consisting of visual, auditory and olfactory impressions, which are storable in memory, usable in dreaming and in unconscious waking thinking" (Symington and Symington, 2002: 61).[12] Segal notes that "the move from beta to alpha and from paranoid schizoid to depressive are conjoined phenomena which are interdependent".[13] Both secondary processing and the alpha function are key aspects of mentalization.

Literary Form

The relevance of the previous discussion about the nature of the P/S and depressive positions is to illustrate the importance of form in the development and enabling of thought. We are *informed* – ideas take on meaning once they become concepts and are expressible in language. It is not until we have clearly articulated a thought or emotion to ourselves that we realize what we have been thinking or feeling. The philosopher R.G. Collingwood[14] argues that the aim of the artist is both to express and understand himself – to clarify the "perturbation or excitement, which he feels going on within him, but of whose nature he is ignorant" (Collingwood 1938, 109). The artist brings to light these unconscious feelings and in doing so gains emotional insight: "As unexpressed, he feels it in what we have called a helpless and oppressed way; as expressed, he feels it in a way from which this sense of oppression has vanished. His mind is somehow lightened and eased" (110). Although Collingwood is not referring to deeply unconscious mental states which are the concern of psychoanalysts, his analysis of the importance of expression for both understanding and working through emotions articulates the work of expression. Before an emotion, or other mental state, is expressed, it remains inchoate – it is a "perturbation or excitement" which lacks a clear outline. We are unable to understand what we are feeling until we conceptualize or categorize our state of mind.

Such reflective activity is the hallmark of mentalization, which characterizes the entry into the depressive position. Klein articulates the importance of language in the development of the depressive position by noting the importance of symbol formation in the development of the self. Segal develops this by distinguishing symbolic representation from symbolic equation:[15] in the latter, word or concept and object are identified, while in the former, which characterizes language, the word or symbol is distinguished from what is represented by it. Symbolic equation is a feature of concrete thinking, while symbolic representation, or "true symbolism", which is also essential for language, is the mark of the depressive position and essential for mentalization. The role of language is thus vital for mentalizing capacities, and abstract thinking would be impossible without it. Works of literature employ language in highly structured ways that transcend the language of ordinary discourse, important though that is for both communication and understanding. Linguistic structure is not a decorative outer covering of an inner state of mind but helps constitutes the thought or emotion it articulates by shaping and providing coherence to inchoate feelings. Some of this structure is found in the formal elements of literature, to which I now turn.

One of the most important psychoanalytic discussions of the importance of literary form is Segal's paper "A Psycho-Analytical Approach to Aesthetics".[16] Here, she explores the origins of aesthetic pleasure, which, she argues, is derived from an identification "with the work of art as a whole" (Segal 1952, 204) rather than with, say, the characters or depicted events. The root of aesthetic pleasure, especially of great works of art, is reparation, and Segal views the formal elements of art as providing the necessary structure and containment to allow for reparation of difficult emotions. Classical tragedy is a prime example of the work that form can do:

> The formal modes of speech, the unities of time, place and action, the strictness and rigidity of the rules are all, I believe, an unconscious demonstration of the fact that order can emerge out of chaos. . . . There can be no aesthetic pleasure without perfect form.
>
> (Segal 1952, 204)

The strictness of the formal elements of a work of art serves to contain powerful emotions by providing a structure that can allow for the processing of emotions. Another way of saying this is that the formal elements of a literary work provide the opportunity for mentalized affectivity. For Aristotle, plot allowed for emotional processing (*katharsis*) via understanding: if events happen *propter hoc* and not merely *post hoc*, this means that there is a structural narrative that can explain how and why the terrible events of the tragedy (*pathos*) occurred. Understanding leads to insight, and then to mastery: if we – unlike Oedipus or Lear or Othello – can articulate to ourselves the things we fear, we may be able to prevent ourselves from falling prey to these unconscious forces. Segal takes this further by suggesting that not only does the audience gain insight into the destruction that may lay in wait for us should we fail to understand ourselves, but she indicates that the audience must experience the full horror of the tragedy in order to make reparation and achieve a state of harmony. Reparation is a central concept for Segal; following Klein, Segal understands reparation as an intrinsic aspect of the depressive position. The infant must not only work through his feelings of guilt aroused in response to his attacks against the good mother, but he must abandon the fantasy of the idealized perfect mother. Acknowledging reality involves accepting that a loved object can be flawed and holding the ambivalence rather than retreating into a phantasy of split objects that are either all-good or all-bad. Working through rather than avoiding painful experiences is key, and aesthetic form is that feature of a work of art that facilitates the process by providing the structures that allow for higher-order thinking, both thinking about thinking and thinking about feelings.

Segal extends the discussion regarding the importance of aesthetic form and the nature of beauty from tragedies to the aesthetic experience more generally. The regularities of form are a key aspect of all art, she claims, and she reworks her account of tragedy into a more general account of ugliness and beauty. Painful and difficult experiences – the ugly – are worked through and overcome via the aesthetic elements of the work of art. Segal is not claiming, of course, that *all* works of art necessarily engage with reparative activity, but she does think that literature especially is well suited to engaging with tragic and painful emotions, and great works of literature derive their status in part from their importance in our emotional lives. She writes: "It is easier to discover this pattern of overcoming depression in literature, with its explicit verbal content, than in other forms of art" (Segal 1952, 206). In poetry, form is perhaps even more important, and the reader's responses are guided by the way the poet structures the imagery and other formal devices in the poem. In addition to the structure of a plot or formal modes of speech, Segal includes the rhythm of speech or music, which is associated with the experience of goodness in rhythmical sucking and breathing, as well as the association with the mother's heartbeat.

Form as Coping Mechanism

The function of aesthetic form in containing difficult emotions is discussed too by the philosophers Susan Feagin[17] and Jenefer Robinson.[18] Although Feagin does not provide an account of tragedy that focuses on form, she notes the importance of metacognitive thinking in our experience of tragic pleasure. The pleasure we feel in response to tragedy as a literary genre cannot be found in the direct responses to the tragic events: there is no pleasure to be taken in watching Othello's torment at the hands of the cunning Iago, or of seeing Lear, no matter how foolish he has been, abandoned by his daughters. Rather, Feagin argues, tragic pleasure is:

> a meta-response, arising from our awareness of, and in response to, the fact that we do have unpleasant direct responses to unpleasant events as they occur in the performing and literary arts. We find ourselves to be the kind of people who respond negatively to villainy, treachery, and injustice.
>
> (Feagin 1983, 98)

Feagin argues that this meta-response brings us a feeling of satisfaction and connection with others: we experience a shared humanity by recognizing our ability to be moved with empathy and compassion to human suffering.

Robinson, like Segal, argues that form functions as a defence against anxiety along the lines of "Freud's concept of 'ego-defences'" (Robinson 2004, 156). Form "manages" our experience of content by enabling a "secondary appraisal" of our initial emotional responses. Robinson argues that literary form acts as a kind of coping device for the wealth of (often powerful) emotions that we encounter in fiction. Such initial emotional responses are termed by Robinson "initial appraisals" and constitute a reader's engagement with the literary work: "if we are to be involved with the content of a literary work, we need to be emotionally stirred by it: we must feel our wants, interests, values, and so on to be at stake in the encounter" (Robinson 2004, 158). Literary form provides the necessary distance to allow ourselves to modify our initial responses to the content of a work in such a way that we are not overwhelmed by these first powerful responses; in this way, form allows us to enjoy painful and difficult texts in a way that real life does not.

Although Robinson gives a nod to Freud, her account is not psychoanalytic, but it is consistent with Segal's analysis of form as necessary for reparation. For Segal, form brings order to chaotic feelings, while for Robinson, form provides the necessary distance for aesthetic pleasure. In this respect, Robinson may be acknowledging Hume's explanation of the pleasure we find in tragic drama. Hume[19] notes the importance of artistic devices in allowing audiences to take pleasure from watching events from which we would derive no pleasure were they to occur in real life. Hume notes that the "extraordinary effect" of the tragic pleasure "proceeds from that very eloquence, with which the melancholy scene is represented" (Hume 1987 [1757], 219). It is the "beauty of oratorial numbers" that "diffuse the highest satisfaction on the audience, and excite the most delightful movements" (220). In other words, Hume argues that the distancing effects of imitation and the pleasure provided by aesthetic devices enable an audience to enjoy tragic fiction.[20] We can understand both Robinson's and Segal's accounts as giving a nod to the importance of mentalizing skills: secondary appraisals are, in essence, higher-order thoughts that enable a reader to step back from the overwhelming content of a work.

Form as Perspective

Formal elements in literature do more than contain or provide structure; they also direct our attention to elements of the narrative and shape a reader's perspective on the depicted events. Narrative voice provides the viewpoint for the reader's attention; the third-person voice, with an omniscient narrator, is perhaps the most common narrative style, followed by the first-person voice. The second-person voice is rarely used. Third-person narration is often regarded as the most reliable, while first person is often associated with the unreliable narrator who either deceives the reader (as in Christie's masterpiece *The Murder of Roger Ackroyd*) or is self-deceived and knows less about himself than the reader eventually does (Humbert Humbert in *Lolita*). But, as James Wood[21] notes, this is not necessarily so – the first-person narrator, as in *Jane Eyre*, may be highly reliable, while a third-person narrator may be partial or misleading. Narrators do not merely report situations as they unfold; they present a perspective from which the reader must infer the intentions of characters and the implications of their actions. Implicit in the narrative function is the communication between the author (or implied author[22]) and the reader: as Deborah Knight notes, narrators are interpreters, and such interpretation involves a three-way relationship "between the narrator and the narrative's central agent, as well as between the narrator and the audience" (Knight 1997, 72). Wood agrees, noting that omniscient narration is rare, as the narrator almost always reveals her partial vision to the reader.

Third- and first-person narration often coincides with Richard Wollheim's account of iconicity of imagination: I may see an event from an external perspective (what Wollheim terms "acentral" imagining) or from the perspective of a character in the scene ("central imagining"). In the latter case, I "successively represent the sights and sounds and smells and internal sensations as they would have reached the eyes and ears and nose"[23] of the person in the scene whose perspective I take. Points of view invite interpretation: sometimes the interpretative activity is relatively straightforward – we accept the words of the author or narrator at face value. This is the case with most fiction, where the emphasis is on the plot and not the inner lives of the characters, such as in pulp fiction, crime thrillers, or romance novels. But the more complex the writing, the more the reader is encouraged to consider the perspective of the author in relation both to the characters *in* the literary work and to the reader *of* the literary work. In Chapter 4 on Jane Austen, I examine her use of free indirect discourse,[24] which is the presentation of first-person perspective via third-person narration. As I hope to show, free indirect discourse is a technique that facilitates mentalization by requiring the reader to reflect on her views about characters and their actions from multiple perspectives, sometimes within a single sentence. Having noted the importance of literary form for mentalization, the next chapters will discuss some examples of this relationship.

Form and Mentalization

The preceding discussion makes the case for the importance of form for mentalization. Mentalization is possible only within the depressive position: the separation of the self from the mother and the external world, the withdrawing of projections, the replacement of primitive defence mechanisms defined by P/S phantasies with mature defences that acknowledge both inner and outer reality – all these are necessary before the capacity for reflection and self-reflection can occur. Because the ability to mourn and make reparation is central to the depressive position, it is a necessary condition also for mentalizing well. "It is only when the loss has been acknowledged and the mourning experienced that re-creation can take place" in the work of art (Segal 1952, 199).

Segal's analysis of aesthetic form as central to creativity is also an argument for the relationship between form and mentalization. This is highlighted in her thoughts about the relationship between art and psychoanalysis: "a psychoanalytic session is an aesthetic experience, because it deals really with the same problem – how to get in touch with terrible things and contain them and sublimate them and lead them to the point of restoration".[25] The form provided in psychoanalysis is the frame of the session, while the forms provided by art are literary conventions. Form contains, enables different perspectives, and makes thinking possible. A piece of clay unworked by the potter is just a clump of earth; by shaping it into a vase or a bowl or a statue of a bird, the ceramicist makes an object that can be used either for practical purposes or admired as an aesthetic object. The same musical notes may be used to create a fugue or a minuet, each with different expressive and aesthetic properties. Form changes what it shapes. This is so also for mental states and processes. It is important to note, though, that, although form structures and contains, it cannot do so rigidly: thinking that is inflexible is antithetical to mentalization. The free play of the mental faculties and flexibility of thought is important not only with respect to the aesthetic. The depressive position is characterized by reparative activity, by the replacement of rigid defence mechanisms with more nuanced and flexible thinking. This is true too for aesthetic form: a poet knows when to alter the metre of a poem, a composer will add an unexpected dissonance in a piece of music – variety and flexibility are always operative, even within prescribed artforms. The next chapters will explore how our ability to reflect on our thoughts and feelings is enabled by different kinds of literary form.

Notes

1 Raymond Williams, *Keywords: A Vocabulary of Culture and Society* (Flamingo, 1983 [1976]): 138.
2 Northrop Frye, "The Four Forms of Prose Fiction", *The Hudson Review* 2, no. 4 (1950): 582–595.
3 David Hume, "Of the Standard of Taste", in *Essays: Moral, Political and Literary*, ed. Eugene F. Miller (Indianapolis: Liberty Classics, 1987 [1757]): 226–249.
4 Immanuel Kant, *Critique of Judgement*, trans. James Creed Meredith (Oxford University Press, 2007).
5 Francis Hutcheson, *An Inquiry into the Original of Our Ideas of Beauty and Virtue* (Indianapolis: Liberty Fund, 2004 [1725]).
6 See, for example, Hume's "Of the Standard of Taste" and Edmund Burke, *A Philosophical Enquiry into the Origin of Our Ideas of the Sublime and the Beautiful* (Oxford University Press, 1990 [1757]).
7 René Descartes, "Meditation Six", in *Meditations on First Philosophy*, trans. Donald A. Cress (Hackett Publishing Company, 1993 [1641]): 47–59.

8 Immanuel Kant, *Critique of Pure Reason*, trans. Norman Kemp Smith (Macmillan, 1985 [1929]): 93 (B 75). By "intuition", Kant means the data of sense experience.
9 Hanna Segal, *Klein* (Fontana, 1979): 64.
10 Donald Winnicott, *The Maturational Processes and the Facilitating Environment* (Karnac, 1990 [Hogarth 1965]): 39 (footnote).
11 Jean Laplanche and Jean-Bertrand Pontalis, *The Language of Psycho-Analysis*, trans. Donald Nicholson-Smith (Karnac Books, 1988).
12 Joan and Neville Symington, *The Clinical Thinking of Wilfred Bion* (Routledge, 2002).
13 Hanna Segal, "Mental Space and Elements of Symbolism", in *Dream, Phantasy and Art* (Brunner-Routledge, 1991): 49–63, at 56.
14 R.G. Collingwood, *Principles of Art* (Clarendon Press, 1938).
15 See, for example, Hanna Segal, "Symbolism", in *Dream, Phantasy and Art* (Brunner-Routledge, 1991): 31–48.
16 Hanna Segal, "A Psycho-Analytic Approach to Aesthetics", *The International Journal of Psychoanalysis* 33 (1952): 196–207.
17 Susan L. Feagin, "The Pleasures of Tragedy", *American Philosophical Quarterly* 20, no. 1 (1983): 95–104.
18 Jenefer Robinson, "The Art of Distancing: How Formal Devices Manage Our Emotional Responses to Literature", *The Journal of Aesthetics and Art Criticism* 62, no. 2 (2004): 153–162.
19 David Hume, "Of Tragedy", in *Essays: Moral, Political and Literary*, ed. Eugene F. Miller (Indianapolis: Liberty Classics, 1987 [1757]): 216–225.
20 I say that Robinson "gives a nod" to Hume because Hume posits a so-called "conversion theory", whereby he argues that painful emotions experienced in response to a work of tragedy are somehow "converted" into pleasant ones. This is not Robinson's position, so the connection to Hume's account of tragic pleasure is only a partial one.
21 James Wood, *How Fiction Works* (Jonathan Cape, 2008).
22 The term "implied author" refers to the "authorial character" who can be inferred as the narrator of the story and who may or may not be identical with the flesh-and-blood author.
23 Richard Wollheim, "Iconicity, Imagination, and Desire", in *The Thread of Life* (Yale University Press, 1984): 62–96, at 73.
24 Otherwise known as free indirect speech, or free indirect style.
25 Jean-Michel Quinodoz, *Listening to Hanna Segal* (Routledge Taylor & Francis e-Library, 2007).

Chapter 3

The Sonnet

The highly structured form of the sonnet provides a shaping principle that allows contained thinking to take place. Without form, thought is not possible, and intricate structures provide for sophisticated thinking. Form enables thought by providing a benign container that is experienced as positive and growth-promoting. Poetry provides for the union of sophisticated thought and powerful emotions in a highly condensed form: a poem of a few lines may express a depth and range of ideas, emotions, and experiences that would require, in prose, a novel to explore.

Similarities between poetry and the development of mentalizing capacities are noted by the psychoanalyst Jeremy Holmes; he writes that both poetry and psychotherapy "regularly arouse suspicion and incomprehension, yet people often turn to them when in states of heightened emotion – love, elation, despair, confusion, loss and bereavement".[1] Holmes also argues that both enhance the capacity for mentalizing: the capacity to "think about feelings" or to be "mind-minded". In exploring the connections between poetry and psychoanalysis, Holmes claims that they enable "reverie", and the "constant interplay between feelings and language" (Holmes 2016, 48). Both poetry and psychoanalysis enable the working through of emotions by using language to give form to unconscious thought and feeling. Of all the literary genres, it is not controversial, I think, to claim that form is of especial importance to poetry: rhythm, rhyme, and structure are central to and constitutive of poetry and delineate it from prose. Poetic form orders and arouses both thought and emotion, providing a unique way for readers to engage in mentalized affectivity. Poets express, in the words of Pope, "what oft was thought but ne'er so well expressed": poetry captures the ineffable of human experience. Poetry cannot be paraphrased or translated without loss: form and content are intricately intertwined, creating an organic unity.

The formal features of poetry are crucial to its meaning. Gordon Graham[2] notes that "if the thought in a poem can be restated in prose without significant loss, it cannot be the poem, strictly speaking, which is directing the mind but only what the poem says" (Graham 1997, 114). This is perhaps true for other literary forms but especially so for poetry, because poetry is expressive not only of ideas but also of emotions, and poetic form is closely tied to how emotions are expressed. For example, the limerick shares with the sonnet the feature of being highly structured.

DOI: 10.4324/9781032702278-4

Spiller[3] notes that the last line of the limerick combines "conclusion with repetition" (Spiller 1992, 4) and functions as "the completion of the narrative, adding an extra item of information but sacrificing the echo, or reprise, of the opening line" (5). The form of the limerick primes the reader to expect "the returning rhythm of the last line to bring with it, like the fifth act of a play, a solution of previous incompleteness" (5). The brevity of the limerick, together with its use of repetition and other stylistic features, arouses in the audience amusement rather than, say, pity or fear. It would be an unusual example of the genre were it employed to express mourning, sadness, or loss: the mismatch between structure and content would jar the reader. Another example where aesthetic form dictates a reader's (or listener's) cognitive and emotional responses is the joke: the philosopher Noël Carroll[4] provides a theory of jokes by examining their "underlying structural principles" (Carroll 2003, 322). He posits that the structure of the joke is strict: "a joke is an integral unit of discourse with a marked beginning and an end" (322), and its distinguishing feature is the punch line, which "concludes the joke with an unexpected puzzle whose solution is left to the listener to resolve" (323). Carroll models his account of jokes on Aristotle's theory of tragedy: just as the formal features of a tragedy are necessary for the arousal of tragic *katharsis*, so too are the formal features of jokes in part responsible for the emotional response (laughter) to which they give rise.

The importance of form in structuring a reader's emotional and cognitive responses is evident too in the sonnet: "compact, shapely, highly finished, and able to contain, in concentrated form, almost all that is human" (Spiller 1992, 1). The sonnet is "probably the longest-lived of all poetic forms, and certainly the longest-lived of all *prescribed* forms" (2, italics in original). A prescribed or closed *form* "is one whose duration and shape are determined before the poet begins to write" (2). Strictness of form primes the reader's expectations. It acts as a container for complex and difficult emotions so that they can be thought about and worked through. The figurative elements of poetry – metaphor, allusion, imagery, rhyme, rhythm, and so on – contribute to its meaning, which results from both form and content. The tight structure of the sonnet is able to convey the development of thought, and its brevity allows the reader to follow and keep in mind, at a single reading, changes in ideas and emotional affect. The sonnet form is thus in a unique position for both depicting and exemplifying the thinking process.

The tight structure of the sonnet form has two main variations: in the Petrarchan sonnet, which is divided into two quatrains and a sestet, the first eight lines (the octave) often act as the development of an argument, and the sestet as its conclusion. In the Elizabethan or Shakespearean sonnet, where the structure is three quatrains and a rhyming couplet, the couplet often takes on the role of presenting a summing up of the sonnet's theme. The sonnet form is also well suited as a vehicle for address: "The sonnet . . . always gives an impression of immediacy, as if it proceeded directly and confessionally or conversationally from the speaker" (Spiller 1992, 5) and is an ideal vehicle for introspective thought. The form also captures a mind in conversation with itself, and the formal structure of both variations "enacts a complication followed by a resolution – an archetype of the common act of problem-solving, or deciding, or even rationalizing".[5] The literary critic Helen Vendler[6] notes that Shakespeare's sonnets are "inward, meditative, and lyrical" (Vendler 1997, 5) rather than "outward, expository, and narrative". The lyric form in the sonnet "gives us the mind alone with itself" (19). Vendler argues that the significance of the sonnet – and of Shakespeare's sonnets in particular – does not necessarily lie in mining the *meaning* of the poem; sometimes a sonnet can be paraphrased as making such banal claims as "I have insomnia because I am far away from you" (13). Rather, Vendler argues that the "appeal of lyric lies elsewhere than in its paraphrasable statement" (14).

What, then, *does* lie at the heart of the Shakespearean sonnet? Wherein lies its value? Vendler argues that great poets use in their sonnets a variety of techniques – temporal, emotional, semantic, dramatic – to allow the development of thought within the tightly knit 14 lines. She argues that one of the ways poetry is able to elicit emotions is by capturing the thinking process that underlies literary creation: "Shakespeare learned to find strategies to enact feeling in form, feelings in forms, multiplying both to a superlative degree" (17). Poetry – and the sonnet form in particular – reveals the evolution of thought in symbolic form; in poetry, thinking is "made visible" (9). Poems may develop arguments, but unlike pure philosophical arguments, poetry appeals to emotions as well as to thoughts and ideas. Indeed, in the best poems, the distinction between a thought and an emotion is an unstable one – mentalizing develops precisely when our cognitive and affective abilities work in harmony.

Shakespeare's Sonnet 30[7]

Shakespeare's famous sonnet illustrates the lyric thoughtfulness of which the form is capable.

> When to the sessions of sweet silent thought
> I summon up remembrance of things past,
> I sigh the lack of many a thing I sought,
> And with old woes new wail my dear time's waste:
> Then can I drown an eye (unused to flow)
> For precious friends hid in death's dateless night,
> And weep afresh love's long since cancelled woe,
> And moan the expense of many a vanished sight:
> Then can I grieve at grievances foregone,
> And heavily from woe to woe tell o'er
> The sad account of fore-bemoanèd moan,
> Which I new pay as if not paid before.
> But if the while I think on thee (dear friend)
> All losses are restored and sorrows end.

The poem represents within its brief length "a multi-layered self, receding through panels of time" (Vendler 1997, 165). Each segment contains a distinct experience of loss, and together they illustrate and capture the process of mourning. An initial period of grief for lost loved ones is renewed, and experienced as though the losses were current. Between these two periods of sorrow, there is an implied hiatus when the mourning process was complete, although it did not bring full resolution. The speaker must re-experience his feelings of sorrow in order to work through the loss in a meaningful way so as to achieve genuine closure.

Like all Shakespeare's sonnets, Sonnet 30 is divided into three quatrains and a rhyming couplet; each quatrain focuses on a particular idea or image, and they are then woven together to form a coherent unity. *Thought* and *thinking* form a central theme. In line 2, the present act of remembering is likened to the summoning of memories before a judge – the critic Stephen Booth[8] notes that "sessions" refers to "the periodic sittings of judges, a court of law" (Booth 2000, 181). The repetition of the "s" sound brings to mind the sweep of judges' robes; it also serves to connect the act of memory ("summon up remembrance") with the vocal ("sighing") and the visual ("seeing"), since "sigh" and "sight" were often confused in Renaissance English. The ability to tie together thoughts and perceptions is a feature of mature mentalizing skills: experiences of sights, sounds, touch, and smell are integrated into a way of seeing the world that provides a sense of enrichment and emotional wholeness. Dimaggio et al.[9] found that patients who suffer "significant forms of psychopathology" (Dimaggio et al. 2012, 1) exhibit disturbances in memory: among other features, their memories lacked "a pictorial quality which might enable a listener to imagine what happened", and memories often lack detail "which would lend an opportunity to understand the memory as a unique experience" (2). Sonnet 30 is characterized by bringing into focus the very *situated* experiences – both emotional and somatic – of the speaker; past losses are expressed through sighing, weeping, moaning, and an eye drowning in tears. These images evoke in the reader a visceral response to the speaker's grief, which can then be processed. The thoughts about old losses bring forth new tears – "with old woes new wail". The alliteration is onomatopoeic – as is the word "sigh" in line 3 – and conjures up the physical sensations of weeping. This also emphasizes the connection between past and current expressions of grief. By engaging imaginatively with the work of mourning, the reader too embarks on an emotional journey with the speaker of the poem.

In line 2 of the sonnet, the speaker does not "remember", but rather "summon[s] up remembrances" – as though the memories are mental states distinct from the subject who remembers. This brings to mind Bion's distinction between "thoughts" and "thinking" – the former term refers to unconscious mental states that are not subject to secondary processing and are unavailable for mentalizing. Only when we are able actively to *think* our thoughts do we start to develop mentalizing skills. It is important to remember that mentalizing capacities are both inward and outward looking – the ability to mentalize refers to our capacity to understand our own minds as well as the minds of others. When thoughts merely *occur* to the mind, the mind is experienced as passive rather than active. To reference Richard Wolheim,[10] "When the mind is passive, thoughts are conceived of as effecting an entry into it, from the outside" (Wollheim 1974, 35), in contrast with an active mind that regards itself as both the source and the location of thoughts. Mentalization, as a metacognitive phenomenon, involves actively thinking about thinking; a mind in which thoughts passively occur is unlikely to exhibit well-developed mentalizing capacities. As the narrative of the poem develops, so too does the speaker's ability to connect different aspects of his past in a way that brings forth a new understanding of his emotional life, as well as a renewed ability to mourn.

Another characteristic of mentalization is the ability to adopt multiple perspectives from which to examine a scenario. This includes the ability to adopt hypothetical perspectives regarding one's own life. In Sonnet 30, the speaker steps out of narrated time to evaluate the actions of his past self. The layered perspectives in Sonnet 30 capture well this aspect of metacognition. The reader of the sonnet, by being required to adopt imaginatively these different perspectives on the speaker's past selves, acquires new emotional insights. A failure to engage in this imaginative work of perspective-taking will result in an aesthetic failure to appreciate the poem: the sonnet asks us to flex our mentalizing muscles via our imagination. At the start of the sonnet, we are presented with a speaker at odds with himself and who, via the act of remembering and the activity of writing, is attempting to achieve emotional resolution. The imagery in the first two stanzas centres on the *eye* and the *mouth*, which do the work of mourning. Perhaps the visual similarity of the open mouth/eye – the "o" – assists with the resemblance. In stanza one, the speaker does not speak but "wail[s]" – an infantile, preverbal expression of sadness. Stanza two is also dominated by oral and visual images: the speaker "drown[s] an eye" for "precious friends hid in death's dateless night". This is a strange image of the eye drowning itself with its tears, as though enacting a kind of suicide. This suggests a strong identification by the speaker with the dead friends – since the dead friends are hidden and can no longer *be* seen, the eye ("I") will refuse *to see*. Midway through stanza two, though, the speaker "weep[s] afresh", which suggests a move back into the present with the capacity to mourn still intact. Here, the eye does not drown itself in tears, but expels grief via the act of weeping: the new experience of weeping does not enact past griefs, but experiences a new sadness, which is expiated rather than endured. Wailing has progressed to "moaning", which seems a more articulate form of grieving.

In stanza three, the relationship between past and present grief is again emphasized via a repetition in the language – the speaker "grieves at grievances foregone", he moves "from woe to woe" to "tell o'er / The sad account of fore-bemoanèd moan", which he "new pays" as if not "paid before". The repetition illustrates how emotions that were experienced in the past are being re-experienced in the present in a way that strengthens and intensifies them. It is not the case that the speaker is simply remembering past griefs; he is re-experiencing and reworking his emotions in the present. This suggests an integration between past and present selves. Note how the emotional movement of the poem is facilitated by its structure – later quatrains are built upon the images and emotional tonality of previous ones and draw the reader forward towards the concluding couplet. There is also a change of imagery – the emphasis on bodily expression via the mouth (sighing, wailing, moaning) and the eyes (seeing, weeping) is transformed to more ego-syntonic activities – grieving and speaking ("tell o'er"). The sonnet which began with "thoughts" ends with "thinking" – lost emotions that were once buried and disavowed have become re-vived, re-experienced, and worked through so that they can be "thought" about.

Sonnet 30 investigates the nature of grief and mourning – its vicissitudes over time, the ways in which it may transform the self and be transformed in turn. By the end of the sonnet, we note how the emotions have transmuted into *meta*-emotions – their object is not only lost loves and deceased friends, but also the past *emotions* of grief and loss. The speaker in Sonnet 30 does not simply give expression to painful emotions, but he reflects on these emotions, and in reflecting changes them. In a short 14 lines, the sonnet expresses and re-enacts the process of mourning – from an identification with the departed loved ones in fantasy, to a more mature kind of grief that has moved from an initial denial to acceptance. The brevity of the poem intensifies the emotional experiences, and the reader inter-weaves the various time-slices of the speaker's multilayered self. The closed form of the sonnet asks the reader to keep in mind a range of emotional experiences and perspectives in a way that a longer poem could not do as effectively. We are induced to identify emotionally with the speaker via imaginatively identifying with his actions. We too are familiar with weeping for dead friends, and feel bereft when we relive old sorrows. The descriptions of grief in the sonnet, immersed in bodily images, have the effect of creating a visceral identification with the speaker. It is via this identification that we can engage in working through these emotions. This ac-count of the reparative aspect of creativity by Hanna Segal captures this idea well:

> The reader identifies with the author through the medium of his work of art. In that way he re-experiences his own early depressive anxieties, and through identifying with the artist he experiences a successful mourning . . . and feels . . . re-integrated and enriched.
>
> (Segal 1952, 204–205)

Although Segal focused on the reparative aspects of creativity, her insights help explain how literary and creative artworks facilitate mentalization. Sonnet 30 both describes and enacts an experience of mentalization, in part via encouraging the emotional identification with the dramatic speaker to which Segal refers. This abil-ity to see from the perspective of another forms a central aspect of mentalizing capacities; the ability to then reflect further upon these various perspectives and subject them to re-examination contributes to the development of higher-order cog-nitive and emotional capacities.

Milton's Sonnet 16[11]

The reparative aspect of poetry and the contribution of poetic form to the contain-ment of emotions is evident especially in poems that deal with grief and mourning.

Milton wrote several famous poems that depict the activity of mourning. Successful mourning requires a working through of grief so that the mourner emerges free
and unburdened and is able to engage fully with herself and others in a newly alive
world. Mentalization is involved in successful mourning. The psychoanalyst Stephen Seligman[12] articulates the connection between mourning and mentalization in
an evocative way:

> Mentalization – having one's own mind – is both a source and an outcome of
> the often painful, but potentially exhilarating, process of becoming available
> to other people, to one's own history and interior life, to one's voice and one's
> actual body, and consequently of life's opportunities and pitfalls.
>
> (Seligman 2007, 342)

We saw elements of this working through in Shakespeare's Sonnet 30, where the
speaker, by the poem's end, has restored his love objects and worked through his
grief. Milton's Sonnet 16, which follows, is also a poem about mourning, as the
poet[13] considers how best to serve God despite his blindness.

> When I consider how my light is spent,
> Ere half my days, in this dark world and wide,
> And that one Talent which is death to hide
> Lodged with me useless, though my Soul more bent
> To serve therewith my Maker, and present
> My true account, lest he returning chide;
> "Doth God exact day-labour, light denied?"
> I fondly ask. But patience, to prevent
> That murmur, soon replies, "God doth not need
> Either man's work or his own gifts; who best
> Bear his mild yoke, they serve him best. His state
> Is Kingly. Thousands at his bidding speed
> And post o'er Land and Ocean without rest:
> They also serve who only stand and wait."

The sonnet is written in the Petrarchan form, in iambic pentameter with the traditional rhyme scheme. The octave is comprised of two quatrains whose rhyming schemes mirror each other: *abbaabba*, and the rhyme scheme of the sestet is
cdecde. The rhyme scheme contributes to the sonnet's meditative quality. Thomas
Stroup[14] notes that the poem is structured like an argument or syllogism: the speaker
asks whether God can expect him to do His work even as He "denies me the light
to work by and even though I desire more than ever to work for him" (Stroup 1972,
244). Patience responds that God does not require his labour: He has many who do
His bidding. Moreover, service to God can take place even with those "who only
stand and wait". The division into octave and sestet reflects the question/resolution
structure of the poem. Stroup further points out that the sonnet is not only in the

form of an argument, but it is also meditative: the meditation as a literary genre "is a spiritual exercise, an interior drama, an examination of conscience, a contemplation, and a consideration" (245).

By the end of the poem, the poet's faith is restored, but this strengthening of his faith has come about as a result of his despair, his questioning of both his devotion to God and of God's love for him. Some interpretations of the poem have seen in the final lines a kind of resignation, an acceptance by Milton of his limitations, and a "beaten-dog"[15] attitude. "The sonnet closes with a firm avowal of resignation", argue Gossman and Whiting.[16] To my mind, this interpretation is difficult to reconcile with both the elegance and craft of the sonnet, and the emotional resonance with which the reader is left by the end of the poem. The highly structured rhyme scheme of the octave requires great skill: the first line of the octave rhymes with the last line of the first quartet, and the first and last lines of the second quartet, while the second, third, sixth, and seventh lines rhyme with each other. Writing a poem of such complexity would indicate significant skill even in a sighted poet. Milton is able to keep in mind the complexity of the rhyme scheme despite not being able to see this rhythmical pattern. This seems at odds with a reading of the poem as indicative of Milton's "beaten-dog" attitude, for surely the poet would recognize the skill of his own handiwork? The contrasting interpretations of the poem as expressing either resignation or worked-through acceptance rest on the weight of the final word: "wait". Does it mean passively doing nothing, in acceptance of one's fate, or is it an indication of the kind of acceptance that ends a period of genuine mourning? Pequigney[17] points out that the line "my Soul more bent" indicates an intensification of Milton's willingness to serve God, and "carries a delicate suggestion of purification by suffering" (Pequigney 1967, 488).

In the octave the poet ruminates on his blindness and grieves that he may not be able to fulfil either his full potential as a poet, or to serve God in the way that is required of him. The language is filled with images of mourning: the world is "dark"; his light is "spent"; his talent, which is "death to hide", is "useless". The octave ends with an angry challenge: "Does God exact day-labour, light denied?" The sestet contains the response. The poet is in dialogue with himself: "a graced and divinely illumined part of his soul answers the complaining query of his previously depressed soul" (Pequigney 1967, 489). Pequigney also points out that there is a change in the poet's relationship with God, "from that of master and servant to that of king and subject" (489). The poet's imagination grows in turn and moves from "the limited confines of a manor to the vast expanse of a kingdom or empire" (489). In the octave, the poet focuses on his grief and loss, and there is an emphasis on the self: *my light, my days, my true account*, and so on. In the sestet, this focus on the self develops into a more philosophical contemplation about the human condition, and references to the self are replaced by more general references to "man", the unnamed "thousands", and "they". The despair and depression of the phrase "dark world and wide" is replaced with the description of an expanse of land and ocean reminiscent of the first days of creation, and the sestet replaces the earlier fear of divine punishment with a confident trust in divine providence.

Christina Pugh[18] notes that, in the short 14 lines of the sonnet, Milton's blind speaker moves from despair to resolution and "the state of being comforted . . . In the course of this reversal, Milton's sonnet exemplifies the centrifugal energies that this highly compressed poetic form both articulates and reins in" (Pugh 2010, 357–358). Pugh notes that the philosophical and theological ideas of this sonnet are sufficiently expansive to be explored in an epic poem, and yet Milton articulates them in this confined form – Wordsworth's "narrow room".[19] Pugh suggests that the sonnet form engenders a particular kind of thinking and simulates the workings of our minds, "particularly when we are ruminating on a problem or issue" (359). The sonnet form makes "the mind secure" (360), even as the speaker is in the grip of a turbulent emotion or is at odds with himself. The turn or change in argument, which takes place after the octave, captures the "logical or emotional shift by which the speaker enables himself to take a new or altered or enlarged view of his subject" (Fussell 1969, 120). We see these meditative elements in both the Shakespearean and Miltonic sonnets; personal grief or loss is worked through by the poem's end, but the resolution is never trite. The heaviness of grief is expressed in both poems as the work of mourning is performed.

The conversational structure of both sonnets reflects the central elements of mature mentalizing skills; a key feature of mentalization is the ability to adopt different perspectives, to take on in imagination the point of view of another, whether that other is another person, one's self at a different point in time, or a hypothetical viewpoint. Shakespeare says it explicitly: "But if the while I think on thee (dear friend) / All losses are restored and sorrows end". In other words, mourning is complete and inner lost objects are restored when one is able to think meaningfully about the significant other. We reconstruct the other as a separate living entity rather than experience him or her as a partial internal object. Our minds develop in consort with others, and the letting go necessary for mourning takes place in a space opened up by our engagement with the minds of others and our own minds.

The short and contained form of the sonnet – Donne's "well-wrought urn" – contains "in concentrated form, almost all that is human" (Spiller 1992, 1). The rigid structure not only provides containment, but it also sets up a rhythm that carries thinking forward. The divisions within the sonnet of either form provide the scaffolding for the development of argument or meditative contemplation: in the Shakespearean sonnet, each quatrain builds on the next and culminates in the rhyming couplet, which may either "sum up" the theme of the poem or provide an ironic turn – or perhaps both. The octave/sestet structure of the Petrarchan sonnet sets up an expectation of a discussion or internal dialogue, and the turn in or around line nine primes the reader to anticipate in the sestet a resolution or dissolution of the concerns raised in the octave. The sonnet is a highly self-conscious art form, and it is thus not surprising that there are sonnets about the sonnet! The sonnet takes itself as the subject of its own musings, just as good mentalization involves thinking about thinking! We thus return to the claims at the beginning of this chapter: form enables mentalization because, in part, thinking is formal. Just as a valid deductive argument form invites logical thinking, so too does a prescribed poetic form invite emotional thinking. Form is the key around which the poet creates the lock and the reader is invited to open the door to gain entrance to the meaning of the text!

Sometimes, of course, form may be purposively disrupted; feelings that overwhelm reason, or emotions experienced as overpowering, may feel uncontained. Form may be experienced as overly restrictive. Bion speaks about the growing foetus that experiences the womb as stifling, as limiting growth, and the baby needs to break free from its narrow constrictions in order to be born.[20] Birth is a release. The breaking of or deviation from form may be emblematic of either chaos or liberation, depending on the situation. Creativity is born in the tension between containment – obedience to form – and liberation – the breaking of convention. All great works of art, including those that adhere to strict classical form, will disrupt the formal elements in order to create meaning or grab the attention of the listener or reader: a poem written in strict iambic pentameter, say, with no variation in the rhythm of the lines, may become boringly predictable to the ear, and a poet will inject a change of rhythm or meter in order to capture the reader's interest or suggest new meaning. Sometimes a poet will work with a particular poetic form in order both to exploit the conventional usages of the form, and to break free from it. In his "Leda and the Swan", Yeats's use of the sonnet form is both conventional and revolutionary.

"Leda and the Swan"[21]

A sudden blow: the great wings beating still
Above the staggering girl, her thighs caressed
By the dark webs, her nape caught in his bill,
He holds her helpless breast upon his breast.

How can those terrified vague fingers push
The feathered glory from her loosening thighs?
And how can body, laid in that white rush,
But feel the strange heart beating where it lies?

A shudder in the loins engenders there
The broken wall, the burning roof and tower
And Agamemnon dead.
                                    Being so caught up,
So mastered by the brute blood of the air,
Did she put on his knowledge with his power
Before the indifferent beak could let her drop?

The poem tells of the mythic rape of Leda by Zeus in the form of a swan. Leda was the mother of Helen of Troy, whose abduction by Paris sparked the Trojan War: a violent conception begets violent events. Violence is a central and clear theme of the poem, and yet the form is a sonnet, a love poem. Form and content seem misaligned; as if to signal this, Yeats presents us with a broken sonnet by introducing a caesura in line 11. The poem is in the form of a Petrarchan sonnet, although the first two quatrains, with their *abab/cdcd* rhyme scheme instead of the more common *abba/abba* rhyme, resemble a Shakespearean sonnet. This creates a division in Yeats's poem between the first and second quatrains of the octave, which is emphasized in the broken line of the sestet. The broken form echoes the "broken wall" and the destruction of Troy. Force and destruction are at the heart of the poem: blow, beat, stagger, helpless, terrified, shudder, broke, burning, dead, brute, drop – the short 14 lines are filled with violent terminology. The poem begins in *medias res*: "A sudden blow": the lyric tradition of the sonnet is cast aside with one forceful gesture as the first quatrain describes the brutal assault by the god on the helpless terrified Leda. Time is suspended: the immediacy of the attack and the overwhelming nature of the physical assault petrify the victim. This is emphasized by the "still" beating of the god's great wings, indicative of timelessness and eternity. The paradox in the phrase "beating still" is suggestive of another division in the poem between the divine and the eternal, and the mortal. The god is all-powerful but motionless (he is still, the girl staggers), and the eternal intrudes into the temporal to disrupt the natural progress of history. The divine being is not ephemeral but physically overwhelming, and the swan, a symbol of love and devotion in another[22] of Yeats's poems, is here a symbol of power and destruction. The word "beating" is repeated in the last line of the octave, in reference to the beating of the heart; there is some lack of clarity with respect to whether the heart is that of Leda or the swan. On one reading, the "strange heart" is that of the god, who is strange and foreign to the helpless mortal. But another reading suggests that the heart may be Leda's: in her encounter with Zeus, she is forever changed, a stranger to her former self. The parallels between Leda and Zeus are hinted at already in the first stanza: "He holds her helpless breast upon his breast". Mortal and god are not that unalike. The final word of the poem "drop" is echoed by the rhyme scheme in the sestet, which "embodies the motion of dropping, as the *efg* descends twice"[23] (Hong 2018, 63).

The poem also depicts a change from Leda's complete helplessness to a position, if not of strength, then at least of ambivalence. "[I]n the first quatrain Leda's resistance to the god is necessarily passive", notes Jane Davidson Reid,[24] but "[w]ith the second quatrain – in a second breath, as it were – she does attempt a struggle", although she notes that "these are eight lines in which the god accomplishes while the girl acquiesces to his dictated will" (Reid 1953, 380). Reid notes a movement from sheer passivity to the beginnings of a struggle, even if unsuccessful. Importantly, the first quatrain is comprised of a set of statements, while the second is constituted by questions: the poetic voice shifts from declarative certainty to interrogative doubt. The questioning continues in the sestet, which unites conception and death, creation and destruction; the divine swan has elements of mortality ("brute blood of air"), and the final question of the poem asks the reader to shift our focus regarding the relationship between Leda and the swan: "Did she put on his knowledge with his power?", the poem asks. The question seems to imply that elements of divine power were indeed transferred to Leda, and the poem asks if, in addition to this power, Leda also gained divine knowledge. The helpless victim of the first quatrain is transformed into a more powerful figure in the final lines. But the transformation is uncertain, and the reader is left with a question rather than a neat resolution.

Uncertainty is a theme of the poem; even the question marks provide a visual association to the shape of the swan's neck. The poem prompts us to ask why a violent rape is written in sonnet form. On one interpretation, the prescribed nature of the sonnet form, with its clearly defined structure and rhyme scheme, provides the perfect container for destructive emotions. Clive Scott[25] notes that "the sonnet works hardest, is perhaps most efficient, when it envisages anarchy, spiritual dislocation, confusion, with that sure-footedness that other forms can hardly approach" (Scott 1979, 11). On one reading, the sonnet form contains powerful, destructive emotions, although the broken line in the sestet indicates that the holding form is pushed to breaking point by the overwhelming nature of the narrative. However, the argument that Yeats chose the sonnet form for this poem because it serves to organize and restrain emotions that are otherwise threatening and overwhelming is countered by the fact that there are many poetic forms he could have chosen. The sonnet is traditionally a love poem, which is seemingly the antithesis of this poem. If we view the sonnet form as integral, not only as a container for powerful emotions but as intrinsically important to the meaning of the poem, we are led to ask whether there are other ways of viewing the violent encounter between Zeus and Leda. Yeats is most definitely not eroticizing sexual violence, and he does not underplay its brutality, and yet he invites us to read more into the poem than that of a description of an assault.

We see in the final lines that Leda's helpless and hapless victimhood is not necessarily as it appears; the poem invites us to consider that, in her encounter with the swan, she gained, perhaps, both knowledge and power. The poem calls to mind myths of poetic inspiration: the artist as the passive vessel through whom the powerful divine muse speaks. It also reminds us of the Annunciation, when Mary accepts her destiny as the mother of God: divine incarnation via a woman's body. "Leda and the Swan" suggests that no immortal gifts bestowed upon humans come without cost. Transcendence and rebirth often involve loss and ruin: "The moment of incarnation, which is the moment of supreme sexuality and creativity, is forced on us as a moment of death and destruction" (Watson 1976, 35) notes George Watson,[26] who writes that, in Yeats's mythology, "the soul *needs* adversity to sharpen its vitality and self-awareness, achieving full definition and form against the background of flux and chaos" (37). This sentiment is stated clearly by Yeats himself in his introduction to his short play *The Resurrection*: "It has seemed to me of late that the sense of spiritual reality comes whether to the individual or crowds from some violent shock, and that idea has the support of tradition" (quoted in Watson 1976, 35). Read from this perspective, Yeats's use of the sonnet form for "Leda and the Swan" suggests that the assault on Leda is also a way in which she grows from the encounter by acquiring qualities of the divine that would, perhaps, have remained otherwise inaccessible. Mortal form cannot contain elements of the immortal without being pushed beyond boundaries defined by space and time, just as the sonnet form is here pushed to breaking point. But the form holds, and the equivocal last sentence of the poem "redirects us to a place of possibility – a question to staunch the flow of disaster upon disaster – as we anticipate this cycle's end and its repercussions" (Hong 2018, 65).

I began this chapter by arguing that the tight structure of the sonnet provides a shaping principle that makes thought possible. Does this imply that a broken form points to the limits of thought? Does "Leda and the Swan" suggest that some experiences are too overwhelming, too traumatic, to be processed in a way that allows for mentalization? The response to this question cannot be a definite "yes" or "no"; on the one hand, the poem, like any other, requires interpretations which engage our mentalizing capacities. We empathize with Leda and experience the assault from her perspective; but we do not remain *within* this perspective, as the poem asks us to consider the meaning of her experiences, both within the confines of the event, depicted in the narrative of the poem, and its wider historical implications. By posing questions to the reader, the poem acknowledges the complexities of this human-divine interaction, and by juxtaposing a violent rape with the traditional lyric sonnet form, the complex interplay between form and content, and the interweaving of meanings, is facilitated. On the other hand, the sonnet exemplifies the ways in which form *can* sometimes appear to constrain ways of thinking and prevent rather than allow for the articulation of thought.

This poem pushes the sonnet form *almost* to breaking point. This "almost" is important because ultimately the form holds: language retains its syntax and structure, there is a clear and consistent rhyme scheme, and the octave/sestet division is in place. But the poem does suggest that new ways of thinking might require new forms of thought. This is certainly the case within genres of art: all artists learn from their predecessors, but invent new ways of *poesis*, of making, and each new style or movement enables new forms of expression. Form that enables mentalizing is adaptable, not rigid; it expands and contracts so as to facilitate the growth of the mind. Yeats's sonnet does not undermine poetic form but illustrates its flexible capacity. What begins with brute physical violence ends with an open-ended question as the *human* form returns to earth after its encounter with the divine. So too, the reader: our encounter with the "complexity of mire and blood"[27] opens up complexities of form and thought that are made possible by the ways in which structure gives shape to new ways of seeing and understanding. Such is the promise of poetry.

Notes

1 Jeremy Holmes, *The Therapeutic Imagination: Using Literature to Deepen Psycho-Dynamic Understanding and Enhance Empathy* (Routledge, 2016): 43.
2 Gordon Graham, *Philosophy of the Arts: An Introduction to Aesthetics* (Routledge, 1997).
3 M.R.G. Spiller, *The Development of the Sonnet: An Introduction* (Routledge, 1992).
4 Noël Carroll, "On Jokes," in *Beyond Aesthetics* (Cambridge University Press, 2003): 317–335.

5 Paul Fussell Jr., *Poetic Meter and Poetic Form* (Random House, 1969): 131.
6 Helen Vendler, *The Art of Shakespeare's Sonnets* (Harvard University Press, 1997).
7 William Shakespeare, *Sonnet 30: When to the Sessions of Sweet Silent Thought*, www.gutenberg.org/cache/epub/1041/pg1041-images.html.
8 Stephen Booth, *Shakespeare's Sonnets* (Yale University Press, 2000).
9 Giancarlo Dimaggio, Giampaolo Salvatore, Raffaele Popolo, and Paul H. Lysaker, "Autobiographical Memory and Mentalizing Impairment in Personality Disorders and Schizophrenia: Clinical and Research Implications", *Frontiers in Psychology* 3 (2012): 1–4.
10 Richard Wollheim, *On Art and the Mind* (Harvard University Press, 1974).
11 John Milton, *Sonnet 16: When I Consider How My Light Is Spent*, www.gutenberg.org/cache/epub/1745/pg1745-images.html.
12 Stephen Seligman, "Mentalization and Metaphor, Acknowledgment and Grief: Forms of Transformation in the Reflective Space", *Psychoanalytic Dialogues* 17, no. 3 (2007): 321–344.
13 Although the poet is not always to be identified with the speaker of the poem, given the reference to his blindness, I identify the speaker of Sonnet 16 with Milton, and use "poet", "speaker", and "Milton" interchangeable to refer to the same person.
14 Thomas B. Stroup, "'When I Consider': Milton's Sonnet XIX", *Studies in Philology* 69, no. 2 (1972): 242–258.
15 E.M.W. Tillyard, *Milton* (Chatto & Windus, 1946): 190.
16 Ann Gossman and George W. Whiting, "Milton's First Sonnet on His Blindness", *The Review of English Studies* 12, no. 48 (1961): 364–372.
17 Joseph Pequigney, "Milton's Sonnet XIX Reconsidered", *Texas Studies in Literature and Language* 8, no. 4, (1967): 485–498.
18 Christina Pugh, "On Sonnet Thought", *Literary Imagination*, 12, no. 3 (2010): 356–364.
19 See Wordsworth's sonnet about the sonnet form: *Nuns Fret Not at Their Convent's Narrow Room*, www.poetryfoundation.org/poems/52299/nuns-fret-not-at-their-convents-narrow-room.
20 Donald Melzer refers to Bion's "birth break" in "The Aesthetic Object", in *Psychoanalysis and Art: Kleinian Perspectives*, ed. Sandra Gosso (Karnac, 2004): 148.
21 William Butler Yeats, "Leda and the Swan", in *Collected Poems* (Macmillan, 1984 [1933]): 241.
22 "The Wild Swans at Coole", which is discussed in Chapter 5.
23 Anna Maria Hong, "Brute Blood: On Reading William Butler Yeats's 'Leda and the Swan'", *Ecotone* 13, no. 2 (2018): 59–65.
24 Jane Davidson Reid, "Leda, Twice Assaulted", *The Journal of Aesthetics and Art Criticism* 11, no. 4 (1953): 378–389.
25 Clive Scott, "A Theme and a Form: Leda and the Swan and the Sonnet", *The Modern Language Review* 74, no. 1 (1979): 1–11.
26 George Watson, "Yeats's View of History: 'The Contemplation of Ruin'", *The Maynooth Review* 2, no. 2 (1976): 27–46.
27 William Butler Yeats, "Byzantium", in *Collected Poems* (Macmillan, 1984 [1933]): 280–281.

Chapter 4

Free Indirect Discourse in Jane Austen

The importance of narrative voice for mentalization is discussed here in relation to Jane Austen's use of free indirect discourse, which is the literary technique whereby the first-person thoughts of the character are written in the grammatical third person. For example, James Joyce's short story "The Dead"[1] begins with: "Lily, the caretaker's daughter, was literally run off her feet" (175). Despite the third-person narration, the reader hears Lily's voice, the ironic "literally" giving a nod to its precise opposite meaning! Free indirect discourse invites the reader to adopt a perspective on the characters other than that provided by the narrator, but the invitation is subtle, and the reader must be alert to its presence.

Free indirect discourse allows for the presentation of a multiplicity of perspectives. It works most powerfully when it provides the author with stylistic flexibility – that is, when a narrator is able to increase or decrease the distance between the omniscient narrative voice and the voices of the characters. This flexibility allows an author of the genius of Jane Austen to comment on her characters, ironically, sympathetically, or satirically, to agree or disagree with their perspectives, to present the voice of one character through the voice of another, and even to tell us what a character is *not* thinking. As the literary critic James Wood[2] notes: "Thanks to free indirect style, we see things through the character's eyes and language but also through the author's eyes and language, too. We inhabit omniscience and partiality at once" (Wood 2008, 11). One of the characteristics of mature mentalizing capacities is the ability to take different perspectives regarding one's own or another's state of mind. Flexibility of thought, viewing a situation or the actions of a person now from this perspective, now from that, are some of the features of being able to mentalize well. As we saw in Chapter 2 on form, thinking that is rigid and inflexible is antithetical to mentalization. This is so because, in part, perspective-taking may provide new information or understanding regarding someone's motivations or intentions, which requires an ability to put oneself in another's shoes, or to understand the motivations of another even as one critically examines their decisions. Austen's use of narrative techniques requires that we pay careful attention not only to the thoughts and actions of a character, but also to the ways in which that character is thought about by others. Another aspect of free indirect discourse, which distinguishes it from reported speech, is that it tends to

DOI: 10.4324/9781032702278-5

preserve the contextual indicators "of the *here* and *now* of the speaker's spatial and temporal perspective";[3] this both emphasizes the characters' perspectives and brings an element of immediacy to the narrative.

Before turning to Jane Austen, by way of contrast, let us examine some other kinds of narrative voices so as to highlight the claim I am defending – namely, that Austen's use of free indirect discourse is valuable for the way it enables superior mentalizing skills and insight of her characters.

> Elizabeth – or Beth, as everyone called her – was a rosy, smooth-haired, bright-eyed girl of thirteen, with a shy manner, a timid voice, and a peaceful expression, which was seldom disturbed. Her father called her "Little Tranquillity", and the name suited her excellently; for she seemed to live in a happy world of her own, only venturing out to meet the few whom she trusted and loved. Amy, though the youngest, was a most important person – in her own opinion at least. A regular snow-maiden, with blue eyes, and yellow hair, curling on her shoulders, pale and slender, and always carrying herself like a young lady mindful of her manners. What the characters of the four sisters were we will leave to be found out.

The passage is from the opening of Louisa May Alcott's classic *Little Women*.[4] It is told from the perspective of the omniscient narrator, who describes the characters and tells the reader about their personalities. The narrator illustrates her warm and affectionate views regarding the protagonists, as the mildly humorous comment regarding Amy's sense of self-importance indicates. Not surprisingly, given that the intended readership is a young audience, understanding the narrative does not require highly developed mentalizing skills – we are not presented with an in-depth analysis of the inner lives of the March sisters – although a capacity for empathy, an interest in and engagement with the minds of others, is clearly required. Omniscient narrators, even reliable ones, bring degrees of insight: the subtlety and sophistication of novelists such as Henry James or E.M. Forster provide the reader with many layers of meaning and insight that require readings and re-readings. Third-person narration usually tells the reader what the characters are doing, feeling, and thinking. By contrast, free indirect speech suggests to the reader what a character is thinking or feeling, at times even without appearing to do so, and often through the eyes of another character. Free indirect discourse opens an interpretive gap in third-person narration into which the reader is invited with our carry case of mind-reading skills.

Persuasion

Jane Austen was one of the first novelists in English to employ the style. She also employs the technique in a unique way. Whereas some other writers use free indirect discourse to replace the authorial voice with the perspective of the characters, so that the author retreats from the purview of the reader, Austen's use of the technique enables her to weave her authorial[5] voice in and out of the narrative, between various characters and their viewpoints. It also provides a method for hinting at the relationship between characters: we may be led to view a situation through the eyes of a character only to realize that this character's perspective is itself shaped by that of another. For example, in *Pride and Prejudice*, the heroine Elizabeth Bennet's harsh judgements against Darcy are influenced greatly by Wickham; she speaks with conviction about Darcy's pride and cruelty, unconscious of the fact that her point of view has been manipulated. In *Emma*, Harriet persuades herself against marrying Robert Martin, mistaking Emma's disapproval of him as her own. Austen uses the technique at times to show the limited perspective of a character: a character may be sure of herself, and yet the authorial voice hints that his or her self-assurance should be viewed with scepticism by the reader.

Free indirect discourse is a subtle technique and may often be missed unless one is alert to its presence. According to Daniel Gunn,[6] free indirect discourse "has often been characterized as innately disruptive and destabilizing – a technique that allows other voices to compete with and so undermine the monologic authority of the narrator or the implied author" (Gunn 2004, 35). But, argues Gunn, these characterizations of free indirect discourse are insufficient and misleading as ways of understanding the novels of Jane Austen, which use free indirect discourse together with "a trustworthy, authoritative narrative voice and which repeatedly intertwine FID with narratorial commentary, sometimes inside of a single sentence" (Gunn 2004, 35). David Lodge[7] illustrates Austen's fine use of this technique in her final completed novel, *Persuasion*,[8] which tells the story of the love affair between Anne Elliott and Captain Wentworth. Anne, who, at 27, is somewhat older than the heroines of Jane Austen's other novels, had been engaged to Wentworth some eight years prior to the start of the novel. She had been persuaded to end their relationship by friends and family, most notably Lady Russell, whom Anne regarded as a mother figure after Anne's own mother's untimely death. Wentworth was a ship's captain; not being a landowner with a stable position in society and a steady income, he was considered an inappropriate match for Anne. The following passage takes place early in the novel; Wentworth is introduced to the reader.

Captain Wentworth had no fortune. He had been lucky in his profession; but spending freely, what had come freely, had realized nothing. But he was confident that he should soon be rich: full of life and ardour, he knew that he should soon have a ship, and soon be on a station that would lead to everything he wanted. He had always been lucky; he knew he should be so still. Such confidence, powerful in its own warmth, and bewitching in the wit which often expressed it, must have been enough for Anne; but Lady Russell saw it very differently. His sanguine temper, and fearlessness of mind, operated very differently on her. She saw in it but an aggravation of the evil. It only added a dangerous character to himself. He was brilliant, he was headstrong. Lady Russell had little taste for wit, and of anything approaching to imprudence a horror. She deprecated the connexion in every light.

(*Persuasion*, chapter 4: 899)

At first glance the passage seems to be written from the perspective of the omnisci-ent narrator, but Lodge points out that it presents the character of Wentworth "from four points of view in succession: (1) the narrator's; (2) Wentworth's own, (3) Anne's, (4) Lady Russell's" (Lodge 2002, 15) Despite his failed prospects, Went-worth is confident he will make his fortune – after all, "He had always been lucky". Anne's positive response to Wentworth is captured by the words "confidence", "powerful", "warmth", "wit". But, notes Lodge, the passage "turns on the second half of the fifth sentence: 'but Lady Russell saw it very differently'. In the rest of the passage, the same characteristics of Wentworth are rehearsed, but differently named and differently evaluated" (16). Lady Russell's influence upon Anne is here subtly conveyed to the reader: no matter what Wentworth or Anne thought about his potential as a suitor, Lady Russell gets the last word. This is confirmed by the next sentence in the novel: "Such opposition, as these feelings produced, was more than Anne could combat." And we are then told: "She was persuaded to believe the engagement a wrong thing." Anne consoled herself by believing that she is doing Wentworth a favour in not accepting his proposal, but their parting is a "misery" to her. The formal style of the narrative in this passage works like a scene in a film that is in deep focus, where foreground, mid-ground, and background are all vis-ible, each layer of perception providing a new interpretation or understanding of the situation, of the ways in which the characters view themselves and are viewed by others.

In *Persuasion*, Austen's use of free indirect speech also highlights the shy and retiring nature of the heroine. She is under the sway of Lady Russell's influ-ence; her mother died when she was only 13, and her father, Sir Walter Elliot, is a foolish and gullible man, a slave to social status, who, by his own admission, does not read. His only interest in books is to see his place amongst the landed gentry. He seems to come to an understanding of himself and his place in so-ciety via external criteria. He is unable to mentalize, to think about his inner world. As the narrator notes: "Vanity was the beginning and the end of Sir Wal-ter Elliot's character; vanity of person and of situation" (chapter 1: 899). Anne is invisible to her family and plagued by self-doubt; she is thus suspectable to the influence of others – open to their persuasions. As the novel tracks her and Wentworth's reconnection, it also traces Anne's growing self-confidence in her own mind. This is reflected in the use of narrative voice as she moves from doubt, self-deprecation, and self-deception to self-understanding and an acknowledgment of her feelings for Wentworth. This self-doubt is reflected in Anne's response to her sister Mary's report of Captain Wentworth's comment about her.

Captain Wentworth is not very gallant by you, Anne, though he was so attentive to me. Henrietta asked him what he thought of you, when they went away, and he said, "You were so altered he should not have known you again".

(chapter 7: 914)

Anne's thoughts are narrated as follows:

> "So altered that he should not have known her again!" These were words which could not but dwell with her. Yet she soon began to rejoice that she had heard them. They were of sobering tendency; they allayed agitation; they composed, and consequently must make her happier.
>
> (chapter 7: 914)

The passage, written in free indirect discourse, captures Anne's attempts to put a positive spin on her feelings of disappointment and mortification in response to Wentworth's comments (or at least, his comments as told by Mary). She tells herself that his words "must make her happier". Mullan[9] notes that Anne is deceiving herself in her attempts to interpret Wentworth's comments in a positive way, and we, the readers, are made privy to her pain. A first reading of Anne's thoughts might lead the reader to think that the judgement about Wentworth is shared by the narrator: Anne *should* give up all hope of reuniting with him because he no longer loves her, he sees her differently because she is "so altered". But once we become aware that this interpretation is Anne's, our view changes, and we realize the psychological skills she uses to avoid pain and loss. This double-take is important because it requires that the reader's own perspective changes so that we become aware that the ways Anne sees herself are not necessarily reflective of how she truly feels. If the passage were written entirely in the third person so that Anne's misunderstandings were apparent from the outset, the reader's empathic stance to her would be diminished. It is because we hear her thoughts *in her own voice* and yet also realize that she is hiding her feelings of loss from herself that our sense of poignancy is heightened. The use of free indirect discourse in this passage enables the reader's dual perspective: we feel *with* Anne, but we can also think *about* her in ways she is, as yet, unable to.

When, by the end of the novel, Anne is able to acknowledge her feelings for Wentworth, her voice and that of the narrator unite. In the following passage, Wentworth notes that Anne is tired, and assists her into a carriage. The passage is written from Anne's point of view:

> Yes; he had done it. She was in the carriage, and felt that he had placed her there, that his will and his hands had done it, that she owed it to his perception of her fatigue, and his resolution to give her rest. She was very much affected by the view of his disposition towards her which all these things made apparent. This little circumstance seemed the completion of all that had gone before. She understood him. He could not forgive her; but he could not be unfeeling.
>
> (*Persuasion*, chapter 10: 928)

The narrator's voice is here at one with Anne's as she becomes aware of Wentworth's love for her. Although her insight is not complete – Wentworth does forgive her – she is moving to a position of self-knowledge that is central in the development of their reunion. Austen could have presented this passage entirely in the third person; in that case, the reader would have been made privy to Anne's thoughts, but we would still need to consider whether the narrative presented an accurate account of Anne's state of mind. By using free indirect discourse, the narrator's perspective is presented simultaneously with Anne's. This dual and harmonious perspective strengthens the reader's sympathy for Anne; it also strengthens our belief in Wentworth's feelings for her. The reader is invited to think about Anne from both an external and an internal perspective; we are also asked to consider the accuracy of Anne's interpretation of Wentworth, as well as our own assessment, as readers, of this interpretation. We recognize Anne's growing insight as well as its limits, and we hope that she will learn to understand Wentworth's feelings for her more accurately. In Austen's novels, the heroine must earn her happiness by achieving a maturity of self and self-reflection. In a fascinating article about sound in *Persuasion*, Kate Nesbit[10] notes that Anne's maturation is reflected too in her confidence as a speaker: in much of the novel, Anne listens rather than speaks, and her ear "remains under the tyranny of others" (Nesbit 2015, 457). As she develops a sense of agency, so she becomes more of an active listener and speaker: "Sound and the spoken word become objects for interpretation and evaluation as her character simultaneously exercises increased independence of thought and action" (460). The acquisition of agency is both a developmental principle and an ethical one. This growth of heart and mind is also a journey for Austen's readers, as we seek to disentangle our views of her characters, and their views of each other: we too must learn to listen with care.

Emma

The use of free indirect discourse to highlight the limits of a character's self-knowledge is on full display in *Emma*.[11] In Emma we are presented with a heroine who muddles in everyone's affairs because she is confident that she knows better, but Emma is a very different heroine from *Persuasion*'s Anne: Anne is much too influenced by others to trust her own mind, while Emma suffers from the opposite problem – she trusts herself too much. Anne has too much doubt, and Emma too little. She suffers from a lack of insight that has serious consequences for those around her. For example, she persuades her friend Harriet to reject a proposal of marriage from a young farmer, Robert Martin, because she, Emma, thinks Harriet can do better. Emma becomes set on marrying Harriet to Mr Elton, despite the inappropriateness of such a match. Emma's own romantic journey culminates in her marriage to Mr Knightley, "one of the few people who could see faults in Emma Woodhouse, and the only one who ever told her of them" (*Emma*, chapter 1: 563). The novel is told from Emma's perspective, and it is testament to Austen's genius that she is able to both adopt Emma's point of view and allow the reader to see how very often that point of view is mistaken. But, like the heroine of the novel, the reader must work hard to distinguish insight from false understanding. In the following passage, a wonderful example of free indirect discourse, the voice of the narrator seamlessly fuses with that of the central character, and the reader must be alert to track the views of Emma from those of the author. In this excerpt, Emma has just revealed to Harriet her error in thinking that Mr Elton was in love with her.

> Her [Harriet's] tears fell abundantly – but her grief was so truly artless, that no dignity could have made it more respectable in Emma's eyes – and she listened to her and tried to console her with all her heart and understanding – really for the time convinced that Harriet was the superior creature of the two – and that to resemble her would be more for her own welfare and happiness than all that genius or intelligence could do. It was rather too late in the day to set about being simple-minded and ignorant; but she left her with every previous resolution confirmed of being humble and discreet, and repressing imagination all the rest of her life.
>
> (*Emma*, chapter 17: 623)

Because the narrative is told from the perspective of Emma, it is vital that the reader distinguish between the narrator's voice and that of her character, because whose perspective we adopt changes how we interpret the passage. Rachel Oberman[12] notes that if we read this passage as authorial comment, "there is an ugly harshness in Emma's opening thoughts" (Oberman 2009, 3), but if we read the sentence "It was rather too late in the day to set about being simple-minded and ignorant" as part of Emma's narrated speech, "it forms a comic beginning to Emma's attempt at self-reform" (3). The sentence "and she listened to her and tried to console her with all her heart and understanding – really for the time convinced that Harriet was the superior creature of the two" is free indirect discourse – it is written in the third person but captures Emma's self-regard at her attempts at consoling Harriet. The phrase "with all her heart and understanding" reflects Emma's own views about her selfless intentions – she seems more concerned with appearing to be generous than with the object of her generosity. Note, however, the author's subtle undermining of Emma's self-satisfaction with the words "for the time" – an indication that Emma's view of Harriet as "the superior creature of the two" is momentary and fleeting, and indeed likely the opposite of how she really feels. Emma's feeling that Harriet is superior is a false modesty aimed at increasing Emma's sense of her own virtue. The final sentence of the extract – "repressing imagination all the rest of her life" – is told from Emma's perspective and indicates her lack of genuine remorse for Harriet's plight; it indicates Emma's view of her meddling in the affairs of others as arising from her lively and creative personality – a product of a youthful imagination rather than, say, a fantasy-prone one. Oberman notes that, in *Emma*, the narrative voice is charming and high-spirited because there is a shared language between the authorial voice and the novel's heroine. As a result, "the reader is often lulled into a false assumption that Emma's and the narrator's voices are interchangeable" (5). This requires the reader to pay careful attention to changes in tone or language so as to be alert to the ways in which the narrator asks us not to accept Emma's viewpoint uncritically, while at the same time alerting us to the persuasiveness of her charm and wit.

Another significant passage that requires the reader to take care in distinguishing between the narrator's voice and that of the character describes the scene where Emma first acknowledges her love for Mr Knightley:

> Emma's eyes were instantly withdrawn; and she sat silently meditating, in a fixed attitude, for a few minutes. A few minutes were sufficient for making her acquainted with her own heart. A mind like hers, once opening to suspicion, made rapid progress. She touched – she admitted – she acknowledged the whole truth. Why was it so much worse that Harriet should be in love with Mr. Knightley, than with Frank Churchill? Why was the evil so dreadfully increased by Harriet's having some hope of a return? It darted through her, with the speed of an arrow, that Mr. Knightley must marry no one but herself!
>
> (*Emma*, chapter 47: 742)

Emma's realization of her own feelings for Mr Knightley is "first described indirectly, from the vantage point of an external narrator, and then presented more directly, as the narrative enters into her mind"[13] (Bray 2001, 18). But because Emma's voice and that of the narrator are interwoven, the reader must tease out where one ends and the other begins. The ambiguity of the narrative also allows for irony: Emma's thought that "A mind like hers, once opening to suspicion, made rapid progress" is self-congratulatory if read from Emma's perspective, but it is an ironic judgement if read from the narrator's perspective. Austen asks that we both empathize with Emma and note Emma's maturation. Indeed, the former is required for the latter: both perspectives are necessary if we are to find Emma sympathetic as a heroine and embark with her on a process of self-discovery. Austen's use of free indirect discourse creates an intimacy between reader and narrator which is often lacking in third-person omniscient narratives. In free indirect discourse, the reader is provided with a lens through which to view the characters: the focus increases and decreases, zooms in or out, each perspective providing a new way of looking either *at* the characters or *through* their eyes. Austen's use of literary technique enables and encourages mentalization not only because it presents different perspectives, but also because it asks us to engage in a variety of ways of thinking and feeling about the characters: textual interpretation facilitates psychological interpretation.

As Emma matures, the narration changes: her speech begins to include the voices and perspective of others "almost as if she has learned the narrative technique that Austen herself uses" (Oberman 2009, 6). She begins to look at herself through the eyes of another and adopts the perspective of the moral centre of the novel, Mr Knightley. In this passage, she chastises herself for her treatment of Harriet:

> Poor Harriet! to be a second time the dupe of her misconceptions and flattery. Mr. Knightley had spoken prophetically, when he once said, "Emma, you have

been no friend to Harriet Smith." She was afraid she had done her nothing but disservice.

(Emma, chapter 47: 740)

Emma's perspective changes from a self-assured, rather self-centred one to one in which she is able to incorporate the voice of another. By the novel's end, the gap between Emma's consciousness and that of the narrator becomes smaller, and Austen's critical ironical voice is less in evidence.

> The joy, the gratitude, the exquisite delight of her sensations may be imagined. The sole grievance and alloy thus removed in the prospect of Harriet's welfare, she was really in danger of becoming too happy for security. What had she to wish for? Nothing, but to grow more worthy of him, whose intentions and judgment had been ever so superior to her own. Nothing, but that the lessons of her past folly might teach her humility and circumspection in future.

(Emma, chapter 54: 773)

Austen depicts Emma's growth in her mentalizing capacities by showing the changes in perspective in her ways of thinking and talking. The complexity and subtlety of her use of free indirect discourse enables her to enlarge or diminish the distance between the voice of the narrator and the characters, as well as the points of view of the characters with respect to one another. Austen recognizes the essentially social nature of human interaction: we develop our minds in response to other minds, and we learn to understand ourselves in part by looking *at* ourselves from the perspective of another. In *Emma*, the narrative voice transitions seamlessly between different characters' perspectives via the use of narrated monologue and free indirect discourse; this implies that, as social beings, our psychologies are inherently interconnected, composed of multiple perspectives and voices. In order to mine as much meaning from the nuance of Austen's writing, we must learn to distinguish the voice of the narrator from those of the characters. Is the narrator being ironic? If she is, is the irony harsh or mild? Is she in sympathy with her characters? Whose voice is this? Austen was very much aware of her readers – she wrote to her sister Cassandra, "I do not write for such dull elves / As have not a great deal of ingenuity themselves".[14] Indeed, Austen asks her readers to approach her books with an ingenuity and wit that, if dull on page one, will hopefully have sharpened by the final pages.

Pride and Prejudice

No discussion of Jane Austen can ignore her most famous novel, *Pride and Prejudice*.[15] Its opening sentence is one of the most well-known and well-loved in all of English literature: "It is a truth universally acknowledged, that a single man in possession of a good fortune, must be in want of a wife" (*Pride and Prejudice*, chapter 1: 171). Austen's humorous irony is on full display. Although the sentence is not written in free indirect discourse, it betrays similar features to this technique by simultaneously presenting two points of view: that of the characters in the novel, and that of the author. For the characters, or at least some of the characters – especially the mothers – the statement functions as a guiding principle for life: wealthy men *should* want to marry, and who better to grant their wish than one of their own daughters. The concerns of marriage and status as a central theme in the novel are presented from the get-go. But Austen's ironic voice lets the reader know that the "truth universally acknowledged" is indeed *not* a "truth universally acknowledged", but rather a form of wishful thinking. The very extravagance of the claim arouses the reader's suspicions, and we are asked to probe further. Lisa Zunshine[16] puts it this way: the sentence

> derives at least some of its ironic punch from the play between its status both as representation and as metarepresentation. This sentence activates in its readers two rather different information-processing strategies, for it is framed simultaneously as an "architecturally true" statement and a statement to be processed under advisement.
>
> (Kindle Locations 1242–1244)

The simultaneous presentation of two, sometimes conflicting, points of view that typifies free indirect discourse is in evidence from the opening line of *Pride and Prejudice*, an indication of Austen's perennial concern with providing layers of meaning for her readers in ways that facilitate metacognitive capacities. But Austen's techniques are always subtle, and the subtlety is part of both the pleasure and the proficiency. Like her characters, we, the readers, must learn to interpret subtle clues and cues: a lingering handshake, an averted gaze, a tone of voice. In Austen's world, understanding the minds of others always involves knowing that the characters' actions are constrained by the social conventions of class, money, and status. This is so too for *Pride and Prejudice*; William Deresiewicz[17] notes that its heroine, Elizabeth Bennet, "cannot appear until well into this initial story because it is that story – the story of how a community thinks, talks, exerts influence – that produces her plot, that produces her" (504).

Regarding plot, it would be helpful for the reader, before proceeding with further discussion of Austen's literary techniques in *Pride and Prejudice*, to present a brief synopsis of the plot. The novel centres around the Bennet family: Mr and Mrs Bennet and their five daughters, Jane, Elizabeth (the heroine), Mary, Catherine (Kitty) and Lydia live on an estate in the village of Longbourn in early nineteenth-century England. Mr Bennet inherited the estate but legally may not bequeath it to his daughters – it must pass to his nearest male heir, Mr Collins. The Bennet daughters' financial security is thus tenuous, and it is important they marry, and, preferably, marry well. Mrs Bennet is thus delighted when Mr Bingley, "a young man of large fortune from the north of England" (chapter 1: 171) moves into neighbouring Netherfield Park. The novel describes the path to his and Jane's eventual union. The focus of the novel, however, is on the second-oldest Bennet daughter, Elizabeth, her father's favourite. Elizabeth meets Mr Darcy, a close friend of Bingley, and although he displays his prideful nature by refusing to dance with her at a ball, he and Elizabeth become increasingly attracted to one another. The villain of the story is an officer named Mr Wickham, whose lies about Darcy turn Elizabeth away from him. Wickham later scandalously elopes with, but does not marry, Lydia. After some twists and turns of the plot, including interference by Darcy's wealthy aunt, Lady Catherine de Bourgh, who considers Elizabeth an unsuitable match for her nephew, the novel ends with the marriages of Jane and Bingley, Elizabeth and Darcy, and, thanks to Darcy's financial support, Lydia and Wickham.

As noted earlier, a sense of community lies at the heart of all of Austen's novels, and especially in *Pride and Prejudice*: the opening sentence expresses the hopes and aspirations not only of Mrs Bennet, but of all mothers of daughters in the neighbourhood. Community shapes character and behaviour: from etiquette to custom, to forms of expression, views, and attitudes. The traditions and mores that shape individuals is a constant theme in Austen's novels. Deresiewicz (1997) points out that in *Pride and Prejudice*, community plays an important role in shaping mental processes. He notes that phrases such as "He was discovered to be proud", "His character was decided", " 'Every body says that", "a report soon followed", and so on reflect not only the norms and customs of society, but also its "cognitive processes" and "mental habits" (Deresiewicz 1997, 504). Darcy is judged as "the proudest, most disagreeable man in the world, and every body hoped that he would never come there again" (chapter 3: 174). Written in free indirect discourse, this sentence reflects not the view of the narrator, but the judgement of those at the ball, and their verdict is regarded by them as conclusive.

Deresiewicz argues that the novel "takes as its point of departure, not customs or conventions, but cognitive processes" (Deresiewicz 1997, 505). He notes that the opening sentence can be rewritten to function as piece of deductive logic: if X is a single man in possession of a good fortune, then X must be in want of a wife. This will hold true for all X, whether it is Darcy or Bingley, or anyone else. If a young man satisfies the antecedent ("Darcy is a single man in possession of a good fortune"), then the consequent ("Darcy must be in want of a wife") will follow with the force of logical necessity, and the views and feelings of Darcy are irrelevant in the face of this deductive logic. Deresiewicz notes that such syllogistic reasoning functions not to facilitate mentalizing capacities, but to prevent them: he terms them "syllogistic mousetraps" (506) and argues that they occur throughout the novel, functioning as reflexive mental tropisms that result in predictable behaviour. Elizabeth must resist the force of these social syllogisms and develop her own mind in opposition to the appeal of superficial gossip; despite possessing a "quickness of observation" (chapter 4: 176), she is not immune to bad judgement.

Elizabeth must also resist the lure of Wickham's cunning and deceitful charm as he poisons her mind against Darcy. Along with "every lady" in the neighbourhood, Elizabeth is initially attracted to Wickham and his "gentleman-like appearance": his looks and demeanour were "greatly in his favour; he had all the best part of beauty, a fine countenance, a good figure, and very pleasing address" (chapter 15: 203). After an evening of dinner and cards, "Elizabeth went away with her head full of him. She could think of nothing but of Mr. Wickham, and of what he had told her, all the way home" (chapter 16, 208). Elizabeth's head is indeed "full of" Wickham, as she allows herself to see others through his eyes. The opening line of the paragraph that contains the sentence just quoted begins: "Elizabeth allowed that he had given a very rational account of it" (208); the "it" here refers to Wickham's opinions of Lady Catherine de Bourgh and Darcy. The passage, although written in the third person, reflects Elizabeth's thoughts and is an example of free indirect discourse. The word "rational" is used ironically: Elizabeth is allowing herself to be persuaded by Wickham's account of Lady Catherine and Darcy, and she engages in a kind of self-deception by lowering her guard and permitting herself to be led astray by Wickham's attractive appearance and acceptance into polite society. It is in part owing to Wickham's lies about Darcy that Elizabeth rejects Darcy's first marriage proposal; Austen's use of free indirect speech presents the episode from Elizabeth's perspective:

> In spite of her deeply-rooted dislike, she could not be insensible to the compliment of such a man's affection, and though her intentions did not vary for an instant, she was at first sorry for the pain he was to receive; till, roused to resentment by his subsequent language, she lost all compassion in anger. She tried, however, to compose herself to answer him with patience, when he should have done . . . she could easily see that he had no doubt of a favourable answer. He *spoke* of apprehension and anxiety, but his countenance expressed real security.
>
> (*Pride and Prejudice*, chapter 34: 255, italics in original)

We see in this passage Elizabeth's inner struggle between her growing affection for Darcy and her anger at him for his treatment of both Wickham and her sister Jane, whose developing romance with Bingley was, she believes, thwarted by Darcy. The phrase "for an instant" suggests an entreaty to herself *not* to change her decision to reject Darcy's proposal – she needs to set her mind *against* him in order to counter her growing feelings *for* him. Elizabeth is also shown to understand Darcy well, and her ability to distinguish between what he says and how he feels illustrates her attunement to him, despite her misjudgements. It also, of course, reveals Elizabeth's capacity for mentalization. The use of free indirect speech in this passage provides the reader with an insight into Elizabeth's deliberations and allows the reader to enter easily into her thoughts.

After being rejected by Elizabeth, Darcy writes her a letter in which he explains his reasons for opposing Jane and Bingley's marriage, claiming that he misunderstood her sister's true nature. He further clarifies the situation regarding Wickham, whom Elizabeth realizes has misled her. We are made aware of the contents of Darcy's letter not directly, but through Elizabeth's reading of it, and we are privy to her change of mind regarding Wickham: she is uncertain who to believe, but in the end trusts Darcy:

> On both sides it was only assertion. Again she read on. But every line proved more clearly that the affair, which she had believed it impossible that any

contrivance could so represent, as to render Mr. Darcy's conduct in it less than infamous, was capable of a turn which must make him entirely blameless throughout the whole.

(Pride and Prejudice, chapter 36: 262)

Elizabeth mulls over the information she has of Wickham and realizes that she knows little of his true nature:

She could see him instantly before her, in every charm of air and address; but she could remember no more substantial good than the general approbation of the neighbourhood, and the regard which his social powers had gained him in the mess.

(Pride and Prejudice, chapter 36: 262)

Elizabeth is now able to distinguish her views from those of the neighbourhood and renounce those "mental habits" that are quick to form judgements based on appearances. Elizabeth's esteem and love for Darcy grows after Lydia's elopement and subsequent marriage to Wickham. She is moved by his anger towards himself for not exposing Wickham's true character sooner, but she fears that he will not wish to be acquainted with any family of which Wickham is a part. In realizing her loss, she is awakened to her true feelings of love for Darcy:

She began now to comprehend that he was exactly the man, who, in disposition and talents, would most suit her. His understanding and temper, though unlike her own, would have answered all her wishes. It was an union that must have been to the advantage of both; by her ease and liveliness, his mind might have been softened, his manners improved, and from his judgment, information, and knowledge of the world, she must have received benefit of greater importance.

(Pride and Prejudice, Chapter 50: 308)

Austen again uses free indirect speech to capture Elizabeth's state of mind. We see her evaluating herself in relation to Darcy – comparing their strengths and weaknesses and realizing that together they would have brought out the best in one another. She thinks about him in relation to herself, and vice versa. Although she does not here explicitly adopt his point of view about her, by acknowledging the ways in which they might each benefit the other, Elizabeth illustrates a depth of understanding that was lacking at the beginning of the novel, when gossip and first impressions[18] formed the basis of her judgements. She is also able to tolerate, indeed celebrate, the differences between herself and Darcy, which suggests a new-found ease in accepting perspectives different from her own.

These developments in Elizabeth's mentalizing capacities are reflected by the ways in which Jane Austen uses free indirect speech: from forming her perspective of Darcy via the views of others to seeing him truly, the linguistic features of the novel trace and reflect to the reader her mental development. We, the readers, must in turn develop our own mentalizing capacities, in part by adopting Elizabeth's perspective, in part by standing back and observing her from a distance. The reader follows the heroine's intellectual and emotional maturation by being made privy to her perspective on the world, but we are also afforded the opportunity to reflect upon and critique this perspective. Free indirect discourse thus allows for great flexibility in the way that an author can express the thoughts of her characters. More than other techniques, it sets up a triangular relationship between reader, writer, and protagonist, whose actions are reflected from a variety of perspectives. The stylistic technique allows too for authorial irony and sympathy. Free indirect discourse thus involves those metacognitive and meta-affective capacities so important for mentalization. In the hands of a writer like Jane Austen, free indirect discourse is also directed at making a reader more sensitive to the moral and social concerns of her characters. Her heroines mature through the course of her novels and learn to understand both themselves and those around them; their attainment of happiness symbolized in a socially sanctioned union. "Mentalization", Jurist[19] reminds us, "is the skill that enables one to interpret others' minds, which developmentally precedes and then fosters the ability to read and understand one's own mental states" (Jurist 2005, 428). Austen's use of free indirect speech shows us that book-reading and mind-reading require similar skills. Creative writers, Freud notes, "are apt to know a whole host of things between heaven and earth of which our philosophy has not yet let us dream. In their knowledge of the mind they are far in advance of us everyday people."[20] If this is true, it is so not only because of *what* great writers write, but, perhaps more importantly, in *how* they write.

Notes

1 James Joyce, "The Dead", in *Dubliners* (Penguin Books, 1976 [1916]): 175–224.
2 James Wood, *How Fiction Works* (Jonathan Cape, 2008).
3 Anne Waldron Neumann, "Characterization and Comment in *Pride and Prejudice*: Free Indirect Discourse and 'Double-Voiced' Verbs of Speaking, Thinking, and Feeling", *Style* 20, no. 3 (1986): 364–394, at 367.
4 Louisa Mary Alcott, *Little Women* (1896), www.gutenberg.org/cache/epub/37106/pg37106-images.html#I.
5 The term "authorial voice" is indifferent between that of the real flesh-and-blood person of Jane Austen, or the implied author.
6 Daniel P. Gunn, "Free Indirect Discourse and Narrative Authority in *Emma*", *Narrative* 12, no. 1 (2004): 35–54.
7 David Lodge, *Language of Fiction* (Routledge, 2002 [1966]).
8 Jane Austen, "Persuasion", in *The Works of Jane Austen* (Allan Wingate, 1962 [1818]): 887–1000.
9 John Mullan, *What Matters in Jane Austen* (Bloomsbury, 2012).
10 Kate Nesbit, "'Taste in Noises': Registering, Evaluating, and Creating Sound and Story in Jane Austen's *Persuasion*", *Studies in the Novel* 47, no. 4 (2015): 451–468.
11 Jane Austen, "Emma", in *The Works of Jane Austen* (Allan Wingate 1962 [1816]): 559–777.
12 Rachel Provenzano Oberman, "Fused Voices: Narrated Monologue in Jane Austen's *Emma*", *Nineteenth-Century Literature* 64, no. 1 (2009): 1–15.

13 Joe Bray, "The Source of 'Dramatized Consciousness': Richardson, Austen, and Stylistic Influence", *Style* 35, no. 1 (2001): 18–33.
14 R.W. Chapman, ed., *Jane Austen's Letters to Her Sister Cassandra and Others* (Oxford University Press, 1959): 297–298.
15 Jane Austen, "Pride and Prejudice", in *The Works of Jane Austen* (Allan Wingate, 1962 [1813]): 169–343.
16 Lisa Zunshine, *Why We Read Fiction: Theory of Mind and the Novel* (Ohio State University Press, 2006), Kindle.
17 William Deresiewicz, "Community and Cognition in *Pride and Prejudice*", *ELH: English Literary History* 64, no. 2 (1997): 503–535.
18 Indeed, the original title for *Pride and Prejudice* was *First Impressions*.
19 Elliot L. Jurist, "Mentalized Affectivity", *Psychoanalytic Psychology* 22, no. 3 (2005): 426–444.
20 Sigmund Freud, "Delusions and Dreams in Jensen's *Gradiva*", *SE* 9 (1907): 8.

Chapter 5

The Mentalizing Function of Memory

Autobiographical memory is shaped and enhanced by mentalizing capacities – the ability to employ higher-order judgements about our own lives shapes the way we think about ourselves, not only in the present, but also in the past. Autobiographical memory, in part by providing a narrative about who we are, is also *constitutive* of our personhood, and so highly developed mentalizing abilities have transformative powers. Researchers believe that autobiographical memory may serve a social function and facilitate our ability to empathize; Susan Bluck[1] emphasizes "[t]he importance of autobiographical memory in developing, maintaining, and strengthening social bonds", which may be "tied to its potential evolutionary adaptive value" (Bluck 2003, 114). What we remember is crucial to our sense of who we are; our memories form the thread that ties our disparate experiences together into a unified identity, a sense of self. There are memories of discrete events about specific times and places – one's first day at school, or one's wedding day, or swimming in a tidal pool at sunset at the end of summer.

As noted earlier in the discussion of Wollheim, we may remember incidents from our past centrally or acentrally. If I centrally remember playing tennis with Martina, it is more likely that I will remember from a first-person perspective what I felt or thought: I may remember feeling annoyed when I missed an easy lob, or joy at my ace on set point. Remembering acentrally is more likely to include a memory *that* this or that took place, but without the first-person perspective: I remember *that* I was disappointed on missing the lob, but I don't recall the feeling of disappointment itself. Regarding perspective-taking, *how* we remember and *what* we remember are intertwined. Our memories of particular incidents in our lives are termed "episodic memory" because they are about a specific event, date, or place. Episodic memory involves an awareness of the self in the experience – "the feeling that 'I was there, I did that'".[2] Episodic memories contribute to what is known as "autobiographical memory", defined as the "phenomenological element of long-term declarative memory concerned with our capacity to recollect our lives".[3] Autobiographical memory grounds a person's sense of identity by creating a narrative about the self; such narratives include reference to memories about specific times and places (episodic memory), but the narrative about the self is not reducible to episodic memory. Autobiographical memory is more than the

DOI: 10.4324/9781032702278-6

sum of its parts, as creating a narrative involves more than stringing together a set or sets of events.

Our autobiographical memories centre around events that are emotionally resonant or important for us; Nelson and Fivush define it as "declarative, explicit memory for specific points in the past, recalled from the unique perspective of the self in relation to others" (Nelson and Fivush 2004, 488). Autobiographical memory weaves together experiences such that a person has a coherent perspective on her life; as Peter Goldie[4] notes, our narrative sense of self

> is present to us not only when explicitly thinking of our past and future or when explicitly engaged in narrative thinking. It is also intricately involved in the way we engage with and think of our present environment and of ourselves and other people.
>
> (Goldie 2012, 119)

Elliott Jurist notes that "autobiographical memory fosters the autobiographical self, that is, a narrative account that weaves autobiographical memories together in a meaningful way".[5] According to the recent psychological literature,[6] autobiographical memory serves three major functions: it provides a sense of personal identity, it enables us to solve problems and plan our future actions because we learn from the past, and it helps us to form and maintain relationships with other people. Remembering consists of more than retrieval.[7] Psychoanalysis shows us that our life events may take on different meanings when viewed from different perspectives: a new interpretation of a past event may alter our understanding of that event in ways that can bring about radical change, and other psychological literature confirms that the regulation of affect is related to the observer perspective from which an event memory is recalled. For instance, participants in a study[8] were asked to change the perspective from which they remembered an event. When they changed from a first-person to a third-person perspective, the emotional intensity of the remembered event decreased. This decrease of emotional intensity did *not* occur when subjects changed their perspective from third to first person. This illustrates that taking a third-person perspective provided the subjects with the necessary distance to modify their emotional responses regarding a remembered event. Seeing an event through new eyes and at a distance helps regulate emotional intensity. In addition, autobiographical memory "is distinguished by reflexivity and by remembering through re-experiencing" (Jurist 2014, 496), which suggests that autobiographical memory extends our consciousness beyond the particularities of an individual event and locates its meaning in a more expanded sense of self. Autobiographical memory is generally also associated with what's known as "Fading Affect Bias", which refers to our tendency to remember positive events over negative ones: the former "retain their emotional intensity longer than negative events",[9] which further suggests that one of the functions of autobiographical memory is to regulate affect, perhaps partly in an attempt to maintain self-esteem.

Impairments in autobiographical memory are associated with various psychological illnesses: research has suggested that many patients with avoidant, dependent, and obsessive-compulsive personality disorders have impaired autobiographical memory, especially in times of stress. Similarly, narratives of patients with borderline personality disorder have frequently been found[10] to be overly general, less often concerned with prototypical life events, and overall less coherent. Girls suffering from anorexia nervosa "showed a massive overgeneral memory effect" that was "not related to the presence of depression or alexithymia but increased with the duration of the disorder".[11] Autobiographical memory in narcissistic personality disorder (PD) differs from the autobiographical memory of the general population, as it is associated with lower levels of Fading Affect Bias, which implies that the ability to regulate affect is lowered in narcissistic PD. Unsurprisingly, people suffering from schizophrenia have an impaired theory of mind, and thus poor mentalizing skills, as well as poor autobiographical memory retrieval; they also have a tendency "to recollect odd or negative events".[12] The link between autobiographical memory and healthy psychological functioning was made too by Freud: in his case history of Dora,[13] Freud noted that "patients' inability to give an ordered history of their life in so far as it coincides with the history of their illness is not merely characteristic of the neurosis. It also possesses great theoretical significance" (Freud 1905 [1901], 16–17). Freud noted that memory may be distorted in various ways, which include the repression of events, as well as "by altering the chronological order of events" (47). Recovery via psychoanalysis restores autobiographical memory:

> It is only towards the end of the treatment that we have before us an intelligible, consistent, and unbroken case history. Whereas the practical aim of the treatment is to remove all possible symptoms and to replace them by conscious thoughts, we may regard it as a second and theoretical aim to repair all the damages to the patient's memory. These two aims are coincident. When one is reached, so is the other; and the same path leads to them both.
>
> (Freud 1905 [1901], 18)

There is thus a link between autobiographical memory, affect regulation, the perspective from which an event is remembered, and general psychological well-being. There is a positive correlation between psychological health and better and more coherent memory recall. This evidence points to a strong link between autobiographical memory and mentalization, and current research bears this out. The psychiatrist and psychotherapist Giancarlo Dimaggio and his colleagues found that patients suffering from schizophrenia, as well as others with personality disorders, not only have poor autobiographical memory, but also

> suffer from a wide array of dysfunctions in thinking about themselves and others. Referred to as dysfunction in metacognition or mentalizing, this includes

difficulties recognizing mental states, correctly naming them and using them in a flexible way as a reliable source of information.

(Dimaggio et al. 2012, 2)

They conclude that enrichment of autobiographical memory may assist with meta-cognitive capacities. Of course, this is not to suggest that autobiographical memory, even in psychologically robust people, is entirely reliable – distortions and gaps in memory happen to us all. The focus in this chapter is less on *what* we remember, and more on *how* we remember: memory can be used defensively, to protect against pain, or to idealize. It can also indicate reparative activity, because how we remember is linked to the ways in which the self is integrated. It is these features of autobiographical memory that will be examined in the course of this discussion.

Stylistic Features of Memory

The link between autobiographical memory and psychoanalytic therapy is discussed by Tilmann Habermas,[14] who argues that impaired autobiographical memory has certain *formal* or *stylistic* features with respect to the taking of perspectives in narratives. Habermas's paper focuses less on the content of narrative and more on their formal aspects, and he argues that one of the ways we can understand the therapeutic work of psychoanalysis is by thinking about the ways in which both analyst and patient construct a shared third-person perspective, which, according to Ronald Britton,[15] is enabled by the resolution of the oedipal conflict. Habermas is interested in the stylistic features of narrative within the psychoanalytic setting and argues that it is via the gaps in narrative that the workings of the unconscious, and especially the failures of healthy mental functioning, are revealed. By examining the stylistic features of narrative, Habermas argues that we can "objectify aspects of mental functioning" (Habermas 2006, 501) because the ways in which a person relates her experiences provides important evidence regarding healthy or impaired states of mind.

Habermas notes certain narrative features of autobiographical memory that involve a shared third-person perspective – elements that are central to mentalizing. Habermas discusses these elements via the narratives of three patients as exemplifying mature, neurotic, or immature defence mechanisms. He analyses different narrative styles in the relaying of past events and classifies them as exemplifying higher- or lower-order defences, a grading he borrows from the psychiatrist George Vaillant,[16] who, in turn, models his account on Freud. Vaillant ranks defence mechanisms from "psychotic" to "mature"; the less developed defences are those that are more aligned to the paranoid-schizoid position, and are less attuned to reality, while more mature defences are more aligned to self-flourishing, attunement to reality, and an integrated self. Mature defence mechanisms are more adaptive and enable a person's ability to cope, while less mature defence mechanisms are rigid and "maladaptive" (Vaillant 1993, 35). Sublimation is a mature defence mechanism, while acting out or dissociation are examples Vaillant gives of immature defence mechanisms.

Another way of making the point is to say that mature defence mechanisms provide for, while immature defence mechanisms mitigate against, the ability to mentalize. Habermas notes that the narrative modes associated with a mature defence mechanism have features that are consistent with mentalizing functions: such narrative styles facilitate the adoption of a third-person perspective and allow for both speculation and uncertainty. The narrator does not distort the perception of others, including the relationship with the listener. The perspective of the narrator is distinguishable from that of the protagonist. This allows for the past to be reinterpreted as it enables the adoption of hypothetical perspectives – a consideration of how things *might* have been, of how oneself or another might have felt if events had turned out differently. There is "often the timeless perspective of a generalized other, as in formulations such as 'Some people could have thought that'" (504). This illustrates that a mature sense of self can abstract away from the particular and is less rigid in its perspective on the world. This flexibility is a key component of mentalization, as noted in Chapter 1.

On the other hand, the narrative mode associated with a neurotic defence mechanism seems to lack third-person perspective: the narrator presents events only from a first-person perspective, and the way in which he talks about his experiences does not allow a listener to understand fully the nature of his experiences or mindset. The narrator is trapped in his own subjective point of view about the past, and the listener is unable fully to comprehend the narrative, which seems to contain discernible gaps. The narrator who uses the mode associated with immature defence mechanisms "almost never speaks of himself as an actor (most often the subject of the sentence is missing) and does not even use mental verbs" (Habermas 2006, 509). There is also a lack of detail, and no information about the motives of the persons involved in the events – either his own or those of others. Dimaggio et al. note that impaired autobiographical memory is associated with descriptions of events that are bereft of detail, especially with respect to perceptual data (visual, auditory, etc.). People's motives tend to be poorly understood and judged according to narrow and often strict rules, and "dialogue among characters is often repetitive and stereotyped" (Dimaggio et al. 2012, 1).

These narrative features of mature, neurotic, and immature defence mechanisms are obviously not exhaustive; rather, they are illustrative of the elements that are characteristic of more and less healthy and adaptive mental functioning characteristic of mentalizing capacities. Narratives that exemplify mentalizing skills will reflect clarity of thought and emotion, non-rigid thinking, the ability to adopt different perspectives on a situation, and to think about the implications of those perspectives. An event in a life is understood as part of a bigger whole – the *propter hoc* of Aristotelian plots. The work by Habermas and others emphasizes that autobiographical memory is associated with a mature self who possesses the features associated with well-developed mentalizing abilities. For Habermas, being aware of the formal features of narration can assist psychoanalysts and therapists in understanding that *how* clients narrate their autobiographies can signal the nature of their defences, as well as give an indication of their capacities for mentalizing.

Autobiographical Memory in Literature

In this chapter, I examine some literary works of or about autobiographical memory to explore how the narrative features of autobiographical memory may work in literary texts. If the formal styles and narrative techniques of autobiographical memory do reflect mentalizing skills, this can provide a valuable tool to literary critics and aestheticians in understanding the relationship between the ways in which literary *style* reflects psychological capacities or facilitates mentalizing skills; this in turn may help us understand how we, as readers, engage with such texts. On the other hand, if literary narratives share central characteristics with the non-literary, understanding the former may shed light on the latter. In this way, fictional accounts of autobiographical memory may provide helpful ways of understanding that how we relate what we remember tells us interesting and important things about our psychological capacities more generally. Examining the narrative features of autobiographical memory may enable interesting conversations between psychoanalysts and literary critics. The discussions that follow will, of necessity, involve cherry-picking, and I examine three different works of literature that deal with autobiographical memory in three different ways. The aim of the discussion will be to illustrate how these works – Yeats's poem "The Wild Swans at Coole", L.P. Hartley's novel *The Go-Between*, and Sophocles' *Oedipus Tyrannus* – reflect and illustrate interrelations between autobiographical memory and mentalizing capacities.

"The Wild Swans at Coole"[17]

Set in Coole Park, Galway, the home of Yeats's friend Lady Gregory, and written in the autumn of 1916, when Yeats was in his early 50s, the poem is a meditation on the temporality of human life, especially as this stands in contrast with the immutability of the natural world.

> The trees are in their autumn beauty,
> The woodland paths are dry,
> Under the October twilight the water
> Mirrors a still sky;
> Upon the brimming water among the stones
> Are nine-and-fifty swans.
>
> The nineteenth autumn has come upon me
> Since I first made my count;
> I saw, before I had well finished,
> All suddenly mount
> And scatter wheeling in great broken rings
> Upon their clamorous wings.
>
> I have looked upon those brilliant creatures,
> And now my heart is sore.

All's changed since I, hearing at twilight,
The first time on this shore,
The bell-beat of their wings above my head,
Trod with a lighter tread.

Unwearied still, lover by lover,
They paddle in the cold
Companionable streams or climb the air;
Their hearts have not grown old;
Passion or conquest, wander where they will,
Attend upon them still.

But now they drift on the still water,
Mysterious, beautiful;
Among what rushes will they build,
By what lake's edge or pool
Delight men's eyes when I awake some day
To find they have flown away?

Yeats's "The Wild Swans at Coole" is an "extraordinary achievement", according to literary critic Marjorie Perloff, who discusses this poem in her paper "'The Tradition of Myself': The Autobiographical Mode of Yeats".[18] She notes that "The Wild Swans at Coole" is "the first of the great autobiographical poems" (Perloff 1975, 531), in which Yeats enters into an imaginative engagement with his personal experiences which express a core aspect of his inner world. She notes that the poem has a cyclical movement "from the present to the past and back to a present that anticipates the future" (531). The speaker measures "his own linear progress against their cyclic movement", and notes the distance between the world of nature, and himself. The swans are both rooted and eternal: they are an intrinsic part of the landscape, comfortable in the "cold / Companionable streams", but are also able to transcend it, leaving and returning in an endless cycle of belonging. Perloff suggests that the final question indicates the speaker's ability to mourn his imminent loss: he is able to "transcend his personal sorrow; he can accept the swans' imaginary flight into a future that will not include his presence" (531).

The narrative form of the poem thus contains many of the attributes associated with mentalizing. The poem begins in the present and immediately engages the reader's senses, especially those of sight and hearing. The line "Upon the brimming water among the stones / Are nine-and-fifty swans" is highly specific and brings to the mind's eye the image of the swans swimming on the lake. But it also makes the reader wonder, "Why is the number of swans important? How did the poet *know* there were 59 swans? Did he count them? If so, why?" In that one line, Yeats manages to link a detailed visual image with a sense of reflection. This mirrors – as the "still sky" is mirrored in the water – the structure of the poem, where Yeats (or the dramatic speaker) is both present in the poem and outside it. The poet presents a piece of episodic memory which is interwoven with other parts of his life – the poem moves between the present and the past and contemplates a future time and place from which the speaker will be absent. The speaker imagines the past from the perspective of the present, and the present from the perspective of the future: he thinks about a time when he will not exist and simultaneously imbues this time with a phenomenology. The questions "Among what rushes?" and "By what lake's edge or pool?" conjure up vivid scenes even as they describe the speaker's absence from those scenes. This double perspective displays the capacity for "thinking about thinking" that typifies highly developed mentalizing capacities. The dramatic speaker also experiences strong emotions that he can label and understand ("And now my heart is sore"), but he is not overwhelmed by them; he is, in psychological parlance, able to regulate his affect.

Perloff writes that autobiographical memories not only record the past, but shape it: memories fall within a pattern of larger meaning. In "The Wild Swans at Coole", the speaker's memories are indicative both of his individual life and of something larger than himself – the relationship between the individual mortal human and the immortal natural world. For Yeats, the swan is a symbol of the divine – explicitly in "Leda and the Swan", which describes the rape of Leda by Zeus in the form of a swan. In this poem, the swans are symbolic of a wider eternal world, and, of course, of love, as swans are known to mate for life. The immanence of the eternal in the natural is illustrated in various other ways. The word "still" is used four times in the short poem, as both an adjective and an adverb: in reference to the "still sky", to the swans that are "unwearied still"; to their passion and conquest that "Attend upon them still" and to the "still water". Water and sky are mirror images of one another, both in the sense that the water reflects the sky, but also in the sense that they share similar features. The use of the adjective "still" describes them both. The sky, the heavens, is the place of the divine and symbol of the eternal, and the water – the home of the swans – is a kind of heavenly representation on earth. The swans are creatures of both worlds – note that "still" means both silent and motionless, and the swans are located in time, but they are also outside time. Indeed, their movement seems to break the bounds of time and space that define ordinary mortals. The swans "wander where they will"; even their nests are characterized by movement: "Among what rushes will they build?", the speaker asks, using a biblical term that alludes to the discovery of Moses by Pharoah's daughter, hinting at the swans' ancient and eternal nature. In the second stanza, the swans depart, "scatter wheeling in great broken rings". The image of the gyre or spiralling vortex is for Yeats a symbol of history, of movement through time: historical periods move in a series of cycles from birth, maturity and decline, and are replaced in their turn by new civilizations that repeat the cycle. The flight of the swans symbolizes the passage of time, the cyclical decay and rebirth that lies at the heart of human endeavour, for both the individual person and the social order. The swans, whose hearts "have not grown old", can escape this earthly cycle, their "clamorous wings" lifting them above mundane concerns, their flight reminding the speaker of his earth-bound nature.

Poetic elements emphasize what the narrative perspective describes: the poem provides a wonderful example of an autobiographical memory that exemplifies many characteristics of mentalization, of mature narrative style. Note that mentalization does not mean overt intellectualization – on the contrary, an ability to reflect on the nature of one's own mind may require, at times, something close to a state of reverie, where, to reference Kant, the imagination and the understanding engage in free play. It seems to me that Yeats's poem enables just that. The speaker reflects on the passage of time; he acknowledges the limits of human existence and expresses appropriate emotions of grief and sorrow regarding these losses. The poem has a haunting quality, imbuing in the reader a sense of contemplation, of reverie. The poet's imaginative engagement with the swans that are able to escape a time-bound existence provides the speaker with a way of both acknowledging and accepting loss while imagining a world beyond it, one not bound by the limitations of mortality.

The Go-Between

Let us now move to a narrative that illustrates a failure of autobiographical memory and provides an example of narrative style that is representative of a less mature, possibly neurotic, defence mechanism. L.P. Hartley's classic novel *The Go-Between*[19] is a novel of memory and about memory: the narrator Leo – now in his 60s – revisits his childhood in an attempt to make peace with it, but because he is unable fully to understand the past, he remains trapped by it, as exemplified in his role as "go-between".

When Leo was 12, he was invited by a school friend, Marcus Maudsley, to spend a summer holiday at Marcus's family estate at Brandham Hall. There Leo meets Marcus's beautiful sister Marian, who is engaged to the socially appropriate Lord Trimingham but is having an affair with a local farmer, Ted Burgess. Leo is used by the lovers, and, willingly but unthinkingly, becomes a go-between for their relationship, carrying messages between them. Leo idolizes and idealizes the adults in his life, and he is devastated when he stumbles on the truth about Marian and Ted, especially since it also shatters his fantasy that Marian may be in love with *him*. Leo is forced by Marian's mother, on his 13th birthday, to reveal the affair between Marian and Ted, the discovery of which has devastating consequences: Ted commits suicide, and Marian enters into a loveless marriage with Trimingham. Leo leaves Brandham Hall and has a mental breakdown from which he never fully recovers. The reader is told about these events years later, as the adult Leo stumbles across his old diary, which forces him to confront his memories regarding his adolescent summer.

For Leo, these past events were traumatic and, as is the case with unworked-through trauma, are not integrated into his view of his life. This vast distance between his youthful and current self is captured in the famous first line of the novel: "The past is a foreign country: they do things differently there." Leo has never married or made much of his life. He says:

> I felt, with a bitter blend of self-pity and self-reproach, that had it not been for the diary, or what the diary stood for, everything would be different. I should not

be sitting in this drab, flowerless room, where the curtains were not even drawn to hide the cold rain beating on the windows, or contemplating the accumulation of the past and the duty it imposed on me to sort it out. I should be sitting in another room, rainbow-hued, looking not into the past but into the future; and I should not be sitting alone.

(Hartley 1997 [1953], 6)

The unworked-through nature of these traumatic past events is further emphasized by the fact that, at the end of the novel, Leo returns to Brandham Hall and meets Marian, now an old woman and a grandmother. Marian once again asks Leo to act as her go-between and to take a message to her grandson, and Leo – against his better judgement – agrees:

With every step I marveled more at the extent of Marian's self-deception. Why then was I moved by what she had said? Why did I half wish that I could see it all as she did? And why should I go on this preposterous errand? I hadn't promised to and I wasn't a child . . . nothing easier than to ring up Ted's grandson and make my excuses. . . . But I didn't.

(261)

Leo is unable to remember the past and is thus doomed to repeat it. His inability to remember is part of his self-deception, his unwillingness to understand fully the implications of Marian and Ted's exploitation of him. He has blamed himself for Ted's death and Marian's subsequent loveless marriage, unwilling to consider that, on the contrary, he was their victim. Even Marian's birthday gift to Leo of a bicycle was a kind of exploitation, as it was given to him to enable him to be a better messenger, a fact that Leo discovers only at the end of the book. Leo "preferred a life-long effort of forgetting over any attempt to come to terms; only by burying 'the explanation of me' could he find a way to live".[20] He asks: "Was it true . . . that my best energies had been given to the undertaker's art? If it was, what did it matter?" (Hartley 1997 [1953], 16).

The novel links Leo's current empty life with the events at Brandham Hall, and Hartley uses an interesting narrative technique to tell the story of Leo's past from the perspective of the older Leo, while at the same time pointing to Leo's inability to fully recover these memories. As a child, Leo kept a diary, and it is the discovery of this diary, some half a century later, that prompts Leo to think about the past. When he first discovers the diary, though, he does not remember it – "I did not want to touch it and told myself that this was because it challenged my memory: I was proud of my memory and disliked having it prompted" (5). The irony is that Leo is unable to remember the salient events that have altered his life. His discovery of the diary opens a road to the past, to that "other country" peopled with foreigners. He has kept the diary in a storage box along with other "relics" from his youth. At first, Leo is unaware what it is, and notes that the diary has a "foreign look" (5). He is unable to "give it a context" and "did not want to touch it". For Leo, the past is buried, untouchable, locked away in a box with other relics from the past. The locked diary is a powerful metaphor of the ways in which Leo has shut down a part of his own mind; his inability to integrate the past into his present self is illustrative of his inability to think about and work through the painful events that have shaped him because he has not managed to work through them. The diary serves as a prompt for the recollection of events that Leo has buried, and via this technique Hartley is able to present the past to the reader while alerting the reader to the unreliability of Leo's memory. The reader is asked to reconstruct Leo's past *for* him, to engage in those mentalizing activities from which Leo has explicitly recused himself. *The Go-Between* is thus not only a novel constructed *out of* memory, but it is a novel *about* memory, and about the ways in which autobiographical memory and mentalization work hand in hand to construct – or not – a complete sense of self. In a sense, *The Go-Between* is *itself* a kind of letter, a message sent from Leo's older self to his younger one, or, perhaps, a letter from Leo to the reader: as such, it represents a failure on his part, just as Marian and Ted's letters were indicative of the doomed nature of their love affair – the gap between what is desired and what is possible.

Stylistically, the novel exemplifies many of the features Habermas notes are operative in a narrative style that exemplifies neurotic defences. The narrative is told mostly from the perspective of the young Leo; although the novel begins and ends in the present, the main story is told from the perspective of Leo as a child. *This* Leo does not understand the ways of the adult world, the manner in which his innocence has been exploited. The narrator is completely caught up in his subjective perspective, in which he remains trapped. Leo never comes to see himself as an actor, an agent, in his life: indeed, his interest in magic is testament to the magical thinking to which he is prone.

Oedipus: Beyond Narrative

One's autobiographical memory is tied to one's sense of self; gaps in memory, especially concerning significant events, or misremembering, impact one's ability to understand oneself. How one remembers is tied to what one remembers. This is highlighted in Sophocles' *Oedipus Tyrannus*, which can be read as an examination of the failure of memory. Schiller reminds us that the play is an analytic tragedy – the movement is backwards, not forwards, and the resolution comes about when events are understood in the proper way. Sophocles reminds us that *a* narrative about our lives – no matter how seemingly coherent – may not be the true narrative of who we really are. Oedipus, famous for his intellect, is nonetheless opaque to himself regarding central issues in his life. Despite believing the warning by the Oracle that he will murder his father and marry his mother, he does precisely that, running towards his fate even as he believes he is running away from it. He solved the riddle of the Sphinx and saved Thebes from its tyranny, but he is unable to solve the riddle of Oedipus, and in so doing he replaces the threat of the Sphinx with the pollution of his own crime. Oedipus misremembers his past not by forgetting important incidents, but by misunderstanding them. He remembers *that* he killed an old man at the crossroads but does not know that he killed his father. He knows *that* he marries a woman old enough to be his mother but not that Jocasta *is* his mother. *Oedipus* is a mystery story, and it is one in which the main protagonist is both hero and villain, detective and criminal. Oedipus could in all likelihood tell a coherent tale about his life, but his tragedy is that *seemingly coherent narratives* may conceal more than they reveal.

Sophocles' play reminds us that autobiographical memory requires *activity of remembering* – understanding the past differently not only shapes how we view these events, but also in turn allows those past events to shape us in the present. In his *Poetics*, Aristotle insists that tragic form should follow a particular shape – events must happen *because of* (*propter hoc*) previous events, and not simply *post hoc*. In his insistence on plot, Aristotle reminds us that narrative coherence is meaningful when it points to a *deeper* coherence, where the truths about our lives – literal, intellectual, emotional – relate to one another. This is the task of analysis: to enable the past to live meaningfully in the present. True reparation takes place when autobiographical memory enables mentalization.

The story of Oedipus raises a deep worry about narratives: in Chapter 1, I argued that narratives make sense of our behaviour. Folk psychological understanding is tied intrinsically to narratives and their structure: we understand a person's motivations for her actions by telling a story about why she acted, and stories are important because they highlight the reasons and causes of action. Mentalizing capacities involve the ability to provide rich and coherent narratives regarding one's own and others' behaviour. But can narratives conceal even as they pretend to reveal? Sometimes stories serve to hide one's true motivations, and the coherence of narrative may provide cover for a deeper inability to make sense of one's life. Richard Wollheim[21] raises this concern in his discussion on the role of unconscious phantasy, referencing Freud's case study of the Rat Man,[22] a patient of Freud by the name of Ernst Lehrs, who was tormented after hearing about a torture that involved the use of rats. Lehrs suffered from a variety of psychological ailments and obsessional behaviours; in one incident, on the day his fiancée was to leave the resort where they were staying for the summer,

> he knocked his foot against a stone lying in the road, and was *obliged* to put it out of the way by the side of the road, because the idea struck him that her carriage would be driving along the same road in a few hours' time and might come to grief against this stone. But a few minutes later it occurred to him that this was absurd, and he was *obliged* to go back and replace the stone in its original position in the middle of the road.
>
> (Freud 1909, 190, emphases in original)

Lehrs tells himself that his replacement of the stone is an undoing of the original irrational act of removing it from the road; he is correcting his initial inexplicable behaviour. However, Freud argues that he is deceiving himself: the second action of replacing the stone is as irrational as that of removing it from the road was. Both represent

> [a] battle between love and hate [that] was raging in the lover's breast, and the object of both these feelings was one and the same person. The battle was represented in a plastic form by his compulsive and symbolic act of removing the stone from the road along which she was to drive, and then of undoing this deed of love by replacing the stone where it had lain, so that her carriage might come to grief against it and she herself be hurt. We shall not be forming a correct judgement of this second part of the compulsive act if we take it at its face value as having merely been a critical repudiation of a pathological action.
>
> (Freud 1909, 191)

In other words, Lehrs's explanation of his behaviour may seem plausible, but its plausibility is in the service of covering up, rather than uncovering, its real motivation. Wollheim phrases it thus: "At each point in the story, Freud suggests, the Rat Man would have explanations of what he was doing that would add up to an overall account of his behaviour that was utterly convincing and false" (Wollheim 1984, 156). Wollheim argues that the structure of narrative is exploited to make irrational behaviour, motivated largely by unconscious phantasy, appear more reasonable than it really is by being incorporated into ordinary belief-desire psychological explanation. Narrative structure, the scaffolding of mentalizing capacities, can also be exploited to provide a façade for irrational behaviour. One of these enabling features is the sequential nature of narrative: as Aristotle argued, sequences of events form a plot when they occur *propter hoc* – because of one another – and not merely *post hoc* – one after the other. The Rat Man's explanation of his returning the stone to the road reverses this, and he replaces a *post hoc* explanation with one seemingly involving *propter hoc*. When he replaces the stone in the road, Lehrs is not undoing a previously irrational action, but he is rather *continuing* the irrational activity. Both removing and replacing the stone are part of the same unconscious "acting out" of his feelings of ambivalence regarding his fiancée. Rationalization replaces rational explanation. Wollheim's point is that the very nature of narrative allows for such replacement precisely because its function is to make sense of behaviour.

Another element of narrative that can be utilized to disguise irrational activity is that of perspective or point of view. In an earlier chapter[23] in *The Thread of Life*, Wollheim notes that iconic mental states typically involve perspective-taking that can be cashed out in terms of a theatrical metaphor: dramatist, actor, and audience. An iconic mental state is one that involves picturing something "in one's mind's eye", as it were. Beliefs are typically not iconic mental states: if I believe that Phoebe is a dog, or that London is the capital of England, I endorse a proposition, but my believing these statements does not typically involve my picturing Phoebe behaving in a dog-like way, or imagining a map of England with London marked as the capital. Memory, on the other hand, can be both iconic and non-iconic: I can remember *that* I sang at a concert when I was five years old without necessarily remembering my performance at that concert. The former would be an example of non-iconic remembering, and the latter an example of iconic remembering. Narrative typically involves both iconic and non-iconic mental states. Iconic mental states involve perspective, and Wollheim notes that these perspectives change depending on the point of view from which the scenes are imagined. He unpacks them via allusion to the theatre: a scene can be imagined from the point of view of the dramatist, the actor, and the audience (*Thread of Life* 65). Each role provides a different way that a scene can be imagined: a dramatist will usually see an event from a third-person perspective (acentral imagining, in Wollheim's terminology), whereas imagining a scene from the point of view of a character implies a first-person perspective on the events. In Chapter 4 on Jane Austen, I highlighted ways in which her use of free indirect discourse enabled various perspectives in imagining a scene. Just as the sequential nature of narrative can be exploited for the purposes of covering over (rather than uncovering) our true motivations, so too can perspective. Wollheim references Freud's account[24] of a common phantasy of many of his patients, that of being beaten as a child. Freud discovered that it was often difficult to get clarity on the exact nature of the phantasy:

> Who was the child that was being beaten? The one who was himself producing the phantasy or another? Was it always the same child or as often as not a different one? Who was it that was beating the child? A grown-up person? And if so, who? Or did the child imagine that he himself was beating another one? Nothing could be ascertained that threw any light upon all these questions – only the hesitant reply: "I know nothing more about it: a child is being beaten."
> (Freud 1919, 181)

Freud gained some success in uncovering the meaning of the phantasies by ordering them chronologically; he did so "by identifying for each phase a characteristic point of view or absence of it, and characteristic repertoires for the dramatis personae" (Wollheim 1984, 96). In masochistic phantasies, the child represents himself as the one who is being beaten, while in sadistic phantasies characteristic of an earlier phase, the child imagines another child being beaten. Changes in point of view reflect the satisfaction in phantasy of various desires such that "switches in mode of imagination, shifts in point of view, changes of protagonist, all of which are possibilities intrinsic to narrative, allow one and the same phantasized event to exemplify competing desires at one and the same moment" (Wollheim 1984, 150). Changes in perspective may thus not necessarily straightforwardly reflect different points of view, but rather are ways in which the satisfaction of desires, especially of competing or incommensurate desires, may be represented in disguise.

If narrative can be exploited in this way such that what appears to be a coherent narrative in the service of understanding behaviour and providing a proper account of actions and intentions is rather a covering up of the expression of unconscious phantasy and motivations, how can we trust narrative? If, as I have been arguing, folk psychological explanation and narrative are constitutive of our mental lives, then does not the fact that narratives can give us false and misleading accounts undermine this claim? My short answer is "no". The reason for this is that it is precisely *because* folk psychological explanation must be given in the form of a narrative that narrative can be exploited, and even undermined. Folk psychology is in the business of providing rational explanation for behaviour: if we are to make sense of our behaviour, we must, in the ordinary course of things, appeal to that language. Indeed, we cannot give a coherent explanation of ourselves in any other way. It is thus natural that when we try to explain our actions, including those that are mysterious or unclear to us, or where our motivations are opaque, we will attempt to provide a coherent account of these actions on pain of giving no account at all. The language of folk psychology, which has narrative at its core, is constitutive of our explanatory schema; we cannot do without it. But this does not mean that all explanations are equal; some capture our true intention, but others attribute false motivations for the sake of coherence, to provide meaning, or for self-esteem. One of the ways we investigate whether the stories we tell ourselves capture the truth is how robust they are: do they buckle and strain under the weight of their content, or do form and content cohere in a way that provides insight and understanding? The Rat Man's account of his replacement of the stone in the road does not, if we examine it closely, really make sense: in the telling of it, Freud notes that Lehrs *felt compelled* to return the stone to the road. Such feeling of compulsion is a warning that not all is at it seems: it suggests acting out rather than intentional action. In addition, the reason Lehrs gives of returning the stone to its previous place in the road is nonsensical: one cannot undo one irrational action by performing another. Even if Lehrs, on reflection, thought that removing the stone from the road was absurd, it was more absurd to return the stone: rather leave it on the side of the road, especially since then there would be no chance of it causing an accident to a carriage. So even though narrative can cover over the ruptures caused by irrationality, cracks will inevitably appear.

As noted earlier, Habermas and others have pointed out that autobiographical memory narratives associated with mature and neurotic mentalizing skills possess distinctive features, to which we can alert ourselves; the discussion of *The Go-Between* attempted to examine some of the ways in which the main protagonist *fails* to remember and ends up repeating. But interpretation is an art, not a science: reading books requires all the skills and sensitivities involved in reading minds. Being alert to the ways in which we can misremember and misunderstand will enable us to understand better and predict our own behaviour and that of others. Mentalizing is an ongoing endeavour.

Notes

1 Susan Bluck, "Autobiographical Memory: Exploring Its Functions in Everyday Life", *Memory* 11, no. 2 (2003): 113–123.

2 Katherine Nelson and Robyn Fivush, "The Emergence of Autobiographical Memory: A Social Cultural Developmental Theory", *Psychological Review* 111 (2004): 486–511, at 487.

3 Igor Knez, "Place and the Self: An Autobiographical Memory Synthesis", *Philosophical Psychology* 27, no. 2 (2014): 164–192, at 166.

4 Peter Goldie, *The Mess Inside: Narrative, Emotion, & the Mind* (Oxford University Press, 2012).

5 Elliot Jurist, "Whatever Happened to the Superego? Loewald and the Future of Psychoanalysis", *Psychoanalytic Psychology* 31, no. 4 (2014): 489–501, at 496.

6 Celia B. Harris, Anne S. Rasmussen, and Dorthe Berntsen, "The Functions of Autobiographical Memory: An Integrative Approach", *Memory* 22, no. 5 (2013): 559–581, at 560.

7 John A. Robinson and Karen L. Swanson, "Field and Observer Modes of Remembering", *Memory* 1, no. 3 (1993): 169–184.

8 Quoted in Takahiro Sekiguchi and Saori Nonaka, "The Long-Term Effect of Perspective Change on the Emotional Intensity of Autobiographical Memories", *Cognition & Emotion* 28, no. 2 (2013): 375–383.

9 Timothy D. Ritchie, W. Richard Walker, Shawnda Marsh, Claire Hart, and John J. Skowronski, "Narcissism Distorts the Fading Affect Bias in Autobiographical Memory", *Applied Cognitive Psychology* 29 (2015): 104–114, at 111.

10 See Giancarlo Dimaggio, Giampaolo Salvatore, Raffaele Popolo, and Paul H. Lysaker, "Autobiographical Memory and Mentalizing Impairment in Personality Disorders and Schizophrenia: Clinical and Research Implications", *Frontiers in Psychology* 3 (2012): 1–4, at 2.

11 Monica Bomba, Mirella Marfone, Elisa Brivio, Silvia Oggiano, Fiorenza Broggi, Francesca Neri, and Renata Nacinovich, "Autobiographical Memory in Adolescent Girls with Anorexia Nervosa", *European Eating Disorders Review* 22 (2014): 479–486, at 479.

12 Rhiannon Corcoran and Christopher D. Frith, "Autobiographical Memory and Theory of Mind: Evidence of a Relationship in Schizophrenia", *Psychological Medicine* 5 (2003): 897–905.

13 Sigmund Freud, "Fragment of an Analysis of a Case of Hysteria (Dora)", *SE* 7 (1905 [1901]): 2–122.

14 Tilmann Habermas, "Who Speaks? Who Looks? Who Feels? Point of View in Autobiographical Narratives", *The International Journal of Psychoanalysis* 87, no. 2 (2006): 497–518.

15 See Tilmann Habermas, "Who Speaks? Who Looks? Who Feels? Point of View in Autobiographical Narratives," *The International Journal of Psychoanalysis* 87, no. 2 (2006): 501.

16 George E. Vaillant, *The Wisdom of the Ego* (Harvard University Press, 1993).

17 William Butler Yeats, "The Wild Swans at Coole", in *Collected Poems* (Macmillan, 1984 [1933]): 147–148.

18 Marjorie Perloff, " 'The Tradition of Myself': The Autobiographical Mode of Yeats," *Journal of Modern Literature* 4, no. 3 (1975): 529–573.

19 L.P. Hartley, *The Go-Between* (Penguin Books, 1997 [1953]).

20 Caleb Crain, "The Undertaker's Art, Exhumed", *The Nation* (April 2002): 29–31.

21 Richard Wollheim, "The Tyranny of the Past," *The Thread of Life* (Yale University Press, 1984): 130–161.

22 Sigmund Freud, "Notes Upon a Case of Obsessional Neurosis," *SE* 10 (1909): 151–320.

23 Richard Wollheim, "Iconicity, Imagination, and Desire," *The Thread of Life* (Yale University Press, 1984): 62–96.

24 Sigmund Freud, " 'A Child Is Being Beaten': A Contribution to the Study of the Origin of Sexual Perversions", *SE* 17 (1919): 175–204.

Index